Don't Break the Rope!

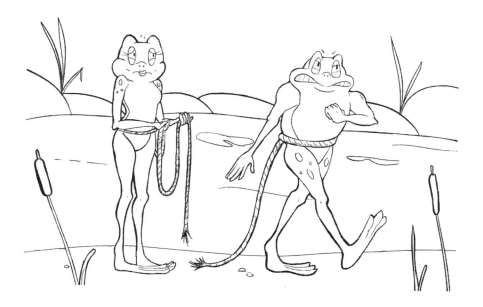

A Parable About Collaboration, Communication and Teamwork in the Workplace

Dr. Erick J. Lauber

Don't Break the Rope!
A Parable About Collaboration, Communication and
Teamwork in the Workplace

ISBN (print) 978-0-9883829-2-3
ISBN (electronic) 978-0-9883829-3-0

Life Framing Intl.
301 S. Third Street
Indiana, PA 15701

Please contact LifeFraming.org

For Betsy, Casey, Emily and Jesse

– Chapter One –

Christopher arrived early at the pond. He wanted to get his stretching routine in before anyone else arrived. It was the morning of the first Challenge at GoodPondInc. He had heard the training and testing program at his new colony was a bit strange, something about a morning swim before beginning the classroom training. He knew he shouldn't be too concerned. He had been captain of the junior swimming team at his old colony, and he was still a fairly young frog. He'd only been in the workforce one year at his old colony before applying to GoodPondInc. But he was still nervous. This was, after all, the best colony on the island. And they didn't keep all of their trainees.

By the time Ashley arrived at the pond, a small group of frogs had already gathered. She felt too nervous to breathe. She hadn't done competitive swimming since before joining her colony's workforce fifteen years earlier. She could tell immediately she was one of the older trainees. It had taken her years to get her application accepted. She was already afraid it had all been for nothing. As she tried to calm herself down, a younger, athletic frog came up beside her.

"So, do you think this will be hard?" asked Christopher.

"Of course," Ashley answered, "don't you? Why would they call it a Challenge if it wasn't hard? And, of course, it would be a swim." As she glanced at Christopher she added, "But you look ready."

"Uh, thanks. I swam a lot in school," he said. "You know … it's just swimming."

"Sure," she said, "but now we get graded for it. I'm older. And you definitely have an advantage with your height."

"Yeah, I guess so. But what has swimming got to do with our jobs in the colony? We're all frogs. We all swim. Why make us race each other? I'm applying to be in the finance department anyway."

Just then, they were interrupted by a shout from a very formal-looking frog. He asked everyone to gather down by the pond's edge.

"First, I would like to welcome all of you to GoodPondInc. My name is Robert and I'll be conducting the morning Challenges for the entire week. I want to congratulate all of you for being admitted to our training and testing program. As you know, after the morning swim, you'll head to the showers and then go to your first classroom training session. Everyone will have lunch together in our cafeteria and, at the end of the day, you are free to get dinner on your own and return to your rooms whenever you like.

"I don't know if anyone told you yet, but the Challenges are a very big part of our testing program here at GoodPondInc. We're not only training you, we're also taking notes on your performance. Not all of you will be asked to stay. I don't want any of you to get nervous about this. It doesn't mean you aren't fantastic frogs and that you won't find great work at another colony. We just have a very particular type of frog we are looking for and not everyone will fit in, or even like working here.

"The Challenges were created a very long time ago and are primarily swimming Challenges. However, there is one unique thing about all of our Challenges: you must complete the swim tied at the waist to another frog."

Both Christopher and Ashley looked surprised. Neither had heard that news. Some of the other frogs began to murmur. Robert immediately spoke up.

"Don't worry," he said. "This isn't nearly as hard as you might think. It does take some coordination, but everyone who works here has done the Challenges, and we're obviously not all equally good swimmers. Before we begin, however, there is one very important point I want to stress before you get in the water. It's vital you finish each swim with your partner. Do not break the rope or untie it, if you can help it. We here at GoodPondInc are very serious about teamwork and we want you to experience very close cooperation with another frog before the training is over. Does anyone have any questions before I describe the first Challenge?"

No one spoke up, but Robert waited a few extra seconds to see if the quieter frogs had something to ask. Ashley's heart raced even faster. She knew she was a decent swimmer, but her small size would make it hard to keep up with even an average-sized frog.

Christopher, on the other hand, immediately began looking over the other frogs. He was assessing who might be strong swimmers, and who he might want to avoid as a partner.

Robert held up his clipboard and continued. "The first Challenge is a rather simple swim. Out near the middle of the pond, you can see a set of lily pads. In a few seconds, I'm going to read off the pairings and then give you a few minutes to tie a rope to both of your waists. On my whistle, you and your partner must swim out to the lily pads, go around them, and return to shore as fast as you can. Each frog in the tandem will receive the same score. The scores will represent the order in which you get back to shore. The last tandems will get the worst scores. Again, once you get your ropes tied, wait for my whistle before you get in the water."

Ashley looked around and saw what appeared to be at least two dozen frogs gathered on the beach. Christopher had already started walking over to grab a rope from the pile near Robert's feet. Everyone was quiet as Robert began announcing names.

Before the whistle blew, Christopher had had enough time with his partner, Buster, to convince himself he wasn't the best swimmer in the group. Christopher decided he would have to do most of the work. Without any hesitation, he rushed into the shallow water while Buster struggled to keep up. As the weeds tugged on the rope between them, Christopher didn't notice Buster found it more and more difficult to keep his head above water.

Soon, the rope began to fray. Out in the open water, Christopher swam harder and harder. He definitely wanted to finish first. But behind him, Buster eventually just gave up trying to swim.

Christopher could tell Buster had stopped swimming because the rope stayed tight even between his strokes. As he rounded the lily pads, the rope suddenly went tighter, as if Buster had grabbed onto the lily pads.

Suddenly, the rope broke.

As Ashley entered the water with Emma, she was having the same problems as Buster. Emma was a larger frog and seemed unaware of Ashley's struggles. Because of Emma's large size, the rope between Ashley and Emma was shorter than it was between many of the other frog tandems. Ashley found herself working hard just to avoid getting punched or kicked by Emma's arms and legs. Eventually, despite Ashley's good speed for being such a small frog, Emma moved out ahead of her. This caused their rope to be tight all the time. It also forced Ashley out of her normal rhythm, and she was getting tired. She was even having trouble catching her breath.

They hadn't yet reached the lily pads when Ashley was finally just gasping for air. With one strong pull on the rope, she managed to get Emma's attention enough to get her to turn around. Ashley treaded water and waved toward shore. Emma seemed completely surprised, but didn't fight her request. Ashley knew she couldn't make it around the lily pads and back to shore with Emma. As they swam back, Ashley noticed the rope was frayed but still intact. As they walked out of the water, they were one of the first tandems to arrive.

When Christopher made it to shore alone, he quickly approached Robert and began to plead his case.

"I'm sorry," Robert said. "It doesn't make a difference which of you yanked on the rope. Clearly you two didn't finish the swim together. That's why your score will be low."

"But I was pulling him," pleaded Christopher. "I can swim much faster than most of these other frogs. I shouldn't be penalized because my partner can't keep up."

"Didn't you hear me say everyone needed to finish the swim with their partner? With the rope intact?"

"Yes," Christopher replied, obviously trying to contain his emotions. "But you said we needed to finish fast. I could have finished it much faster if I hadn't had a partner."

"Of course," Robert said. "But that wasn't the point."

Christopher wasn't happy, but he didn't want to push his case too far. He didn't know what position Robert held in the colony and he didn't want to make him too mad on the first day. Christopher turned away and silently went to sit down by himself at the edge of the group. He could see Buster was just as mad as he was and was clearly getting the same answer from Robert. At least, Christopher thought, he had finished way ahead of *Buster*. That should count for something.

Ashley was still drying off when Emma had calmed down enough to confront her. "What happened?"

"I couldn't keep up," Ashley explained. "I was trying, but you're just a faster swimmer."

"Yeah, but why did you pull on the rope and make us head to shore?"

"I'm sorry. I was just too tired. I couldn't even catch my breath."

"Really? We hadn't even made it to the lily pads yet!"

"Yes. I'm sorry," Ashley said. She was afraid to bring up how many times Emma had kicked and splashed her throughout the swim. She certainly didn't want to get anyone mad at her the first day. Besides, she thought, why didn't Emma notice she was struggling to keep up? How could Emma not see she wasn't getting enough air? Ashley felt herself getting madder and madder, but she was careful not to let Emma see it.

As Ashley repeated how sorry she was, Emma went off to join a bunch of other frogs. It seemed everyone in the group was complaining about their partners. Robert was making notes on his pad and constantly fielding questions and complaints. When the last tandem arrived, he gathered the frogs together and made a brief announcement.

"As you can see, this Challenge isn't as easy as many frogs think it is. If you look around you'll see over half of the ropes are broken and many of you didn't complete the Challenge. But, don't panic yet. We do not dismiss any frogs on the first day. However, maybe you learned something here today. Go back and think about what happened this morning, and come prepared tomorrow to do something different. Every day you will be tied to another frog, and we expect improvement. The Challenge will always be: can you complete the task, and keep the rope intact, with any one of these frogs as your partner?

"For the rest of the day, you will be in the classrooms receiving your formal orientation to GoodPondInc. For now, go find the showers and I'll stick around if anyone has any last questions."

The group was mostly silent as they headed back to the training building. Christopher wondered to himself what kind of training this was. Was the goal to get every frog mad at each other? Or feel like failures? How would any of this make the colony better?

As Ashley walked, she was only thinking of how mad she was at Emma. Yeah, maybe she should have told her a little bit more about what she was going through. But how come Emma hadn't asked? At least, she thought, the rope stayed intact … thanks to me.

As they walked into the shower building, both Ashley and Christopher had the same thought: tomorrow, they needed to do much better – or their time at GoodPondInc would be very short.

––––––––––––––––

At lunch, Christopher and Ashley sat together at a table with trainees and experienced employees. The conversation naturally turned to the Challenges, and both Christopher and Ashley let out their frustrations. Most of the experienced colony members expressed sympathy and words of encouragement.

As lunch broke up, most of the table went back to work, but one very senior member of the colony stayed at the table. He was slight but athletic looking, and his bald head was in sharp contrast to the big gray mustache just above his big smile. He asked Christopher and Ashley if they had time for a quick conversation, and they both eagerly agreed.

"Great," he said. "My name's Eddie. I've been at GoodPondInc a long time and I thought I might offer you some advice, if you want to hear it."

They both replied, "Of course."

"The Challenges are tough," he said. "Nobody in the colony will argue that. We've all been through them. Learning to do a tandem swim is difficult, but it gets better with practice. I heard you talk about how the morning went and I want to repeat the message Robert probably shared with you. The task is important, but so is the rope. Every day, here at the colony, we have to give equal weight to getting our work done *and* doing it in a way that keeps our relationships strong with other frogs. Learning to tandem swim is a great way to figure out how to work together even outside the water. I'm very proud to work here. At GoodPondInc, there will always be team projects – always tough conversations and group decision making. So, if you don't mind me asking, Christopher, why did you swim so hard, even if you knew it would pull on the rope?"

"I wanted to finish fast," said Christopher, defensively. "What else was I supposed to do? Swim slow?"

"Hmm. I believe you'll have to put some thought into that," Eddie said. "So you see it as either swim slow, or swim fast and break the rope … "

"Of course," Christopher replied. "But I didn't know it would break. Why didn't he just let me pull him? He yanked on the rope and that's what broke it!"

But instead of answering him, Eddie turned to Ashley and surprised her with a question. "So what was it like to have a rope pulling you through the water?"

Ashley didn't answer. She didn't want to make Christopher mad. She could see that what she had been through was just like what his partner, Buster, had gone through. The silence got uncomfortable.

Finally, Christopher said, "Go on."

"It didn't feel good," Ashley said quietly.

"I wouldn't think so," Eddie replied. "Right, Christopher?"

It was Christopher's turn to go silent. Eventually, he blurted out, "But did you break your rope?"

"No," Ashley said. "I tried really hard not to break the rope. But I couldn't keep up. And she didn't even try to look at me or ask me how I was doing." A bit more defiantly, she went on. "My face was being pulled under water. I couldn't even catch my breath!"

"Oh," Christopher said. "I … I didn't know that." Thoughtfully, he added, "My face didn't get pulled under at all." Then he went silent.

Eddie finally spoke again. "Christopher, you didn't realize how your swimming affected your partner. You were just focused on getting it done fast. Ashley, I know this isn't easy, but it might help Christopher if you said more about how that swim went for you."

Ashley continued explaining, but she tried to make it clear she was only talking about Emma, not Christopher. "I remember feeling like I was having trouble getting air. Eventually, it was all I could think about. I wasn't thinking about the swim, or the Challenge. I was only worried about getting air."

Eddie said he understood. He explained that a lot of teamwork could turn in to worrying about air if one teammate felt the other didn't respect their decisions or opinions. If a frog makes it clear they don't think the other one has any skill, or could help in any way, the other frog feels disrespected. It might start off as just annoying, but eventually it becomes very serious. The disrespected teammate starts thinking of nothing else and focuses on getting respect. This is similar to how Ashley felt during the tandem swim. She just wanted air.

Christopher looked up. "You mean respect is like air in the tandem swim?"

"Yes," Eddie said. "Working with someone in a work situation is like swimming with them. You have to take turns, you have to coordinate, and if one frog is not respecting the other, it is all the other frog can think about."

"I have to say, that sounds about right," said Ashley, quietly.

"The tasks we do in our colony are almost never solved by one frog," Eddie said. "It always takes two or more of us. That's why we value our relationships with each other so highly. Some of us even believe the rope is more important than the task in the Challenges. If a choice has to be made between completing the task efficiently, or keeping the rope intact, many in our colony would choose the rope."

"Umm. That's a new idea to me," Christopher said, trying to be respectful. "In my old colony, I was always rewarded for my *own* performance. In fact, most of us hated group work. It never seemed everyone did the same amount of work. And I usually felt the group grade was wrong or unfair."

"There probably never will be a time when you think everyone did the exact same amount of work, or even the same type of work in GoodPondInc," Eddie said. "But that can't make you unwilling to do group work. Nearly everything we do is group work, one way or another. And even though there might be a time when you think breaking the rope is the best decision for that particular task, keep in mind that the colony rarely thinks so. Breaking a relationship with someone means it will be very hard for you to work together next time. And there will always be a next time. Keeping the rope intact is in the best interest of the colony – on almost all occasions – even if it doesn't feel like it's in *your* best interest on some particular day."

"OK. So keeping the rope intact should be my first lesson," said Christopher.

"It's usually most frogs' first lesson," said Eddie. "Didn't a lot of the tandems break their ropes on the first day?"

"They sure did," said Ashley, then quietly, "though not Emma and me."

"Yes, but how much did you really contribute to your swim

when you were struggling to get air?" Eddie asked.

"Not much," Ashley replied. "So, that's another lesson we should learn from the Challenges: getting air is important."

"Yes, I believe so," Eddie said as he began to get up from the table. "I'm sorry, I have to get going. You shouldn't be panicked about how well you did on day one. There are still a lot of Challenges to get through. However, it might serve you well if you wrote down the lessons you wanted to remember as you went along. Learning from the tandem swims each day is certainly one of the objectives of the training."

"Of course," Christopher said.

"Sure," said Ashley. "But what did you mean, 'How much did I actually contribute to the swim?' Do you mean I may have done something wrong?"

"I apologize," Eddie said. "I don't really have the time to explain that right now. But we'll try to talk tomorrow. Just think about it until then. Good luck, both of you. I really want good frogs to join us here at GoodPondInc. I think you both can be great members of our team."

Christopher and Ashley said goodbye and felt a little bit better about what they had gone through that morning. After a long silence, Ashley pulled out a pen and suggested they find a way to write down their lessons before they forgot them. Christopher grabbed some dried lily pad napkins from the middle of the table. He said their first lesson should be: "Don't break the rope!"

"Oh, I completely agree," Ashley said. "But how about we add 'because it's only tandem swimming if you both arrive together.'"

Christopher agreed and they both added it in smaller letters beneath "Don't break the rope!" Ashley then suggested a lesson she really hoped Emma would learn someday. "Everyone needs air."

"Of course," Christopher said, "but everyone knows that. What I think Eddie said about respect being equal to air is really important. I had never thought of it like that before. Maybe we could add something to that lesson. How about: 'Respect is like air: if you don't get it, it's all you can think about.'"

"Oh, great addition," Ashley agreed. She wrote it underneath

"Everyone needs air."

As they headed off toward the classroom training, they each said something encouraging to the other. Then Christopher said, "I've got to call my fiancée and tell her about this."

"Oh, great," Ashley said. "You getting married soon?"

"Well, not until we can afford it," Christopher replied. "That's why I'm so interested in working at GoodPondInc. This is really my first chance to prove myself. And get into a better paying job."

"Well, I'm sure you'll do fine," Ashley said. "I wouldn't worry about it. You're a great swimmer."

But as she walked down the hall she thought, how could he let the rope break? Clearly, keeping the rope intact was the most important part of the Challenge. Why didn't he pay better attention to his teammate?

Meanwhile, Christopher was thinking, what kind of frog is Ashley that she wouldn't just let Emma pull her? Or ask her to swim differently so she could breathe? She knew the goal was to be fast. How was she helping if Emma did all of the work?

As each entered their classroom, they both thought: the other seemed nice but it would be tough to swim with them. So, what would happen when they had to swim together?

– Chapter Two –

On the second morning, Ashley and Christopher arrived at the pond's edge and noticed everyone appeared to have survived the first Challenge. It seemed Robert was telling the truth. No one was cut on the first day. But would that happen again today?

As the last frog arrived, Robert announced that the Challenge would be different this morning. As they could see, three lily pads were spread out in the water. Each tandem had to start by swimming the crawl stroke to the first lily pad, swim the breast stroke to the second lily pad, the backstroke to the third lily pad, and finally the butterfly stroke back to shore. Again, each team's score would be determined by the rank order of how fast they reached the shore. He would announce the teams, give them time to tie their ropes, and then everyone would start when he blew the whistle.

Christopher was feeling nervous as Robert read out the pairings. He knew he was better than average on all of the strokes, but he was again worried about which frog he would be paired with. Some of the frogs looked like they could barely swim every frogs' favorite stroke, the breast stroke. He was particularly troubled by the two lessons he had remembered to read that morning: "Don't break the rope!" and "Everyone needs air. Respect is like air: if you don't get it, it's all you can think about." He knew this meant he would have to slow down and go at whatever pace his teammate could handle. He was afraid that could mean his tandem would finish last.

Meanwhile, Ashley was feeling a bit better about the Challenge that day. She felt she was pretty strong at all of the strokes, but particularly the backstroke. She had won backstroke swimming competitions at her old colony. It was a hard stroke for most frogs and she had practiced it a long time as a young frog. As she waited for her name to be called, she felt confident because at least for part of the swim she would really be helping. And, she thought, at least her face wouldn't be dragged through the water during the backstroke.

As the other frogs gradually found their partners and started tying ropes around their waists, Christopher and Ashley finally heard their names called out – together. They were going to have to partner up for this Challenge. Both of them thought, "Oh, crap," but were careful not to show it.

As they tied the rope around their waists, Ashley and Christopher chatted politely. They both wanted the swim to go well, but they also wanted their budding friendship to have a good start. There wasn't anything romantic starting between them. Ashley was easily ten years older and Christopher had said he had a fiancée. But each liked the conversation they'd had at lunch the previous day. Neither, therefore, brought up their fears about swimming with the other.

When the whistle blew, both began running for the water and dove in simultaneously. It became quickly apparent that Christopher was stronger than Ashley at the crawl stroke. He gradually pulled out ahead. Eventually, she started to feel a tug on the rope every time Christopher pulled his arm through the water.

At least it doesn't feel quite as bad as swimming with Emma, Ashley thought. But still, she was getting pulled out of her natural rhythm. Occasionally she coughed on a bit of water when the tug came unexpectedly. As they approached the first lily pad, she could tell Christopher had started to pause between strokes. This gave her a better chance of keeping up. But still, she couldn't quite get alongside of him. Soon, all of her attention was focused on trying to keep the rope slack.

When they reached the first lily pad, they both grabbed ahold and caught their breath for just a few seconds. Christopher spoke first and asked how she was doing. He said he was surprised at how tired he was. Ashley smiled and simply waited for Christopher to start the next leg of their journey. She didn't notice that about half of the other frog teams were ahead of them and about half were behind. But Christopher did. Mentally he kept track of the other teams. He knew they'd have to keep up the pace if they were not going to fall to the back of the pack.

As they let go and started swimming the breast stroke, again Ashley found she had a hard time keeping up. Christopher's long legs made his kick much more powerful than hers. She was again feeling tugs on the rope within a few strokes.

Because of his concern about their speed, and because the first leg of the swim seemed to go pretty well, Christopher paid less attention to Ashley and concentrated on swimming as fast as he could. She hadn't said anything at the lily pad, had she? Soon he felt the rope tug backward every time he kicked his legs, but he thought to himself "Well, at least I'm helping her along. And she'll tell me if I'm swimming too fast."

Unfortunately, behind him, Ashley was gasping for air. Within a few strokes, she had actually stopped swimming the breast stroke and was doing what many frogs called the "tadpole paddle." She felt like a brand new swimmer, doing everything she could just to keep her head above water. Eventually, the back of her body started sinking in the water and she could feel she was more or less being dragged through the water. But she didn't care. She needed air. She began tapping Christopher's foot when his leg was extended. She tried to get him to slow down, but he didn't seem to notice. She started worrying a lot about whether the rope would break.

When they finally got to the second lily pad, both of them were exhausted. Christopher was mad because they were at the back of the pack. But Ashley thought he looked mad because she had made him do all of the work. She wondered what he might do if she made him even madder. Clearly, she thought, he's capable of breaking the rope. He did it yesterday with Buster. So she decided against offering to take the lead on the next leg of the swim, the backstroke. Instead, she decided she would just concentrate on keeping the rope as slack as possible. In her mind, she calculated it was very unlikely he was faster than her at the backstroke. But, she thought, if she went faster, then she might start tugging on *his* rope. This worried her a lot. What if he got mad and decided to break the rope for that reason? Or what if he stopped swimming, and made her do all of the work? She was afraid of breaking the rope, so, instead of offering to lead, she waited until Christopher seemed ready to go. Pretty soon, they set off on the next part of the swim.

After only a few strokes, Christopher discovered Ashley was pretty good at the backstroke. She seemed to glide through the water very easily. However, Christopher was splashing and struggling to breathe while on his back. He knew, unfortunately, they were not making good time. He saw a couple of teams pass them by and it seemed like a very long time before the third lily pad bumped into the back of his head.

After grabbing the lily pad and filling his lungs with air, he realized he hadn't felt a tug on his rope the entire time. He gave a tired smile at Ashley and was glad he hadn't had to pull her along. As he motioned for them to head toward shore, he tried to feel confident. Though every frog found the butterfly stroke the hardest, at least he knew their rope was intact. A bit stretched and frayed in places, but Ashley seemed quite calm and willing to follow. Perhaps this part of the swim would be easy on him.

During the swim toward shore, Ashley again felt like her face was being pulled into the water every couple of strokes. Christopher was clearly leading the team and didn't seem too concerned that the rope was pulling her under. She felt bad every time she had to stop and tread water just to get some air. She knew Christopher would get mad that she was slowing them down, but she felt like she had no choice. She started to resent that her efforts didn't seem appreciated. How come he wasn't offering to take turns? She knew she would have, if she had been the stronger swimmer.

As they came out of the water, she was surprised to find that roughly half of the teams were ahead of them and half behind. And somehow their rope had stayed intact. But she then started to get concerned about her friendship with Christopher. She quickly untied herself and started apologizing to him about how sorry she was that she hadn't helped the team more.

Meanwhile, Christopher was focused on how far back they had finished. He knew he wasn't doing a very good job of hiding his frustration, but he presumed Ashley was feeling the same thing. Her apologies made it clear to him she wanted to take responsibility for their poor finish, so he tried to make the best of it. He made some remarks about how some of the teams had two male frogs and, "That just wasn't fair." He also said if the whole swim had been just the backstroke, they could have won. He was glad they hadn't broken the rope, so he tried to sound comforting as he told her, "At least we followed the number one rule: don't break the rope."

Ashley, however, could sense Christopher was faking a good attitude. She convinced herself that this was because deep down inside he was really blaming her for their poor finish. This thought made her madder and madder, but she was certain she couldn't show any of this to Christopher. So she tried to fake a smile and pretend that she and Christopher had really done all right.

But she wondered if their friendship could survive this test of "their rope?" Would their relationship break after this one bad experience?

They went off to lunch separately. Each tried to convince themselves, quietly in their heads, that they wouldn't be cut from the program.

At lunch, Ashley looked for a seat at Eddie's table. She found one and waited until most of the other frogs were gone before she found the courage to ask him what he had meant by his comment the day before. She reminded him he had asked her to think about how much she was really contributing to the tandem swim. She explained that she took great pride in avoiding arguments with other frogs. Hadn't it been she who had kept the rope intact both mornings? Eddie patiently listened to her explain and then gently asked her a few questions.

"Do you think it's possible Christopher, and maybe Emma, didn't realize how much you were choking and struggling with air during the swims?" asked Eddie.

"Maybe," she replied. "They both had their back to me, and both were very focused on how hard they were swimming. But why didn't they turn around and check on me? They could easily feel the rope tugging on them. I know that's what I would have done."

"Maybe they thought they were helping out?" said Eddie. "If the tandem was going to swim faster than the slowest swimmer, then maybe they thought the faster swimmer had to pull the slower swimmer?"

"Sure, we may have been going a little bit faster," replied Ashley, "but I was struggling with air. They were ignoring me, and nothing I did seemed to matter. It was like it was all about them and only their efforts and contributions mattered. And certainly what they were doing was hurting the rope, not helping it. What if it had broken?"

Eddie asked, "Of course that would have been bad. It seems you were very concerned about the rope. Why didn't you stop and explain this to them?"

Ashley replied, "Well, you don't just say to someone in a race that they're swimming too fast."

Eddie said, "Why not?"

"Well, because it would have been rude. And they would have gotten mad."

"But look at the alternative," Eddie said. "You got dragged through the water and felt resentful about what they were doing. And they probably got extra tired from tugging on the rope. Did you have a conversation with either of them after the swim, about how you felt?"

"No," she said. "We were polite to each other, but I didn't tell either of them I had a hard time breathing. I could tell they were already unhappy. But I still don't understand why they weren't worried about the rope. Christopher's rope broke the very first day … "

"In my experience," Eddie interrupted, "there are some frogs who put the task ahead of the rope – ahead of their relationships with co-workers. That isn't necessarily a bad thing. Some emphasis on the task is important. But do you mind if I ask you another question? Why didn't you lead when you got to the backstroke?"

"Well … " she said hesitantly, "I didn't want to make him mad. He seemed pretty certain he should lead … though it seemed obvious to *me* that I was better at the backstroke. Why didn't he ask me to lead?"

Eddie said, "Why didn't *you* ask?"

"Well … " she replied, "he had been the leader. He should have asked me to lead. I don't ask to be in charge."

"Why not?" he asked.

"I don't know," she said very quietly. She wasn't very comfortable talking about this topic.

"Well, that could be an issue – with you," he added. "See, if you never lead and never tug on Christopher's rope, several things have to eventually happen. First, you are making Christopher do all of the work – at least most of it. And that can be exhausting – for him. Plus, if it happens often enough, it can just turn into the assumed arrangement. Christopher may come to think he is always supposed to lead.

"Also," Eddie continued, "this arrangement clearly doesn't sit well with you. You say you found yourself feeling like you were dragged through the water. Didn't this happen the most when you actually stopped swimming?"

"Yes. Technically. But it wouldn't have made a difference. Christopher was going to pull me along anyway."

"Well, imagine if Christopher had deliberately and consciously allowed you to lead for a while, for example during the backstroke. Wouldn't that have been better for your team in the long run?"

"Yes, I think so. But why didn't he do that?"

"I don't know. I haven't talked to him. However, I do know one thing. The only frog's behavior you can actually control is your own. Is there something you can do next time to make the situation better?"

"Well, I guess I can actually ask Christopher to let me lead," Ashley said, reluctantly.

"Of course!" Eddie replied, with enthusiasm. "But that does take courage. By the way, do you realize you're having no trouble talking about all of this with me? But I'm not the one you need to talk to, right?"

"Ugh," said Ashley, as she put her head in her hands. "You mean, of course, I should have this conversation with Christopher."

"Sure. You don't want him to think you hold your breath when you're near the person you have to work with, but gladly tell your complaints to other frogs, right?"

"No. No. I don't want anyone to think that." Ashley finally looked up. "I know what you're saying."

"OK," said Eddie. "So let's do something about this. Would it help if you spoke to Christopher with me in the conversation?"

Ashley looked up eagerly. "You bet it would."

"Good," Eddie said, looking over her shoulder. "I can see him right now entering the cafeteria."

As Christopher scanned the room, he saw Eddie and Ashley off at a table by themselves. He felt a mix of anxiety and relief. He had enjoyed sitting with Ashley yesterday at lunch, and he knew Eddie could answer a few of his questions about the swim that morning. But he also felt nervous about approaching Ashley. He didn't know how she felt about their tandem swim. If she was anxious or mad, she seemed pretty good at hiding it. And one question was bugging him more than any other. Why didn't she lead during the backstroke? Certainly she could see he was exhausted. And anyone could tell he wasn't very good at that stroke. Didn't she want to win the Challenge?

Eddie gestured Christopher over to join them. Christopher put on a smile and took his food over.

"Hi, Eddie. Hi, Ashley. How is the fly casserole today? I'm famished."

"Great," Ashley said. "I wondered where you were. Lunch is almost over."

"I was just getting in a few laps at the pond," said Christopher. "I felt bad about our swim this morning, so I decided I would go work on a few things."

"That's great," Eddie said. "But if you are worried about passing the Challenges, it isn't really about how fast you swim, Christopher. It's about how fast you swim as a team."

"Umm, I know," Christopher said. "But I can't think of anything else I can do to help. I really want to be in this colony. And now I'm getting nervous."

"I'm sorry," said Ashley. "I should have helped more this morning. I don't know why I didn't do very well."

"Now wait," said Eddie. He suddenly looked annoyed, catching Ashley and Christopher both off guard. "You just got done telling me what happened this morning, and I didn't hear anything at all you needed to apologize for."

"Umm. Well, we didn't do very well. And Christopher is a faster swimmer than me. So clearly I was holding him back ... "

"No. That's not what happened," said Eddie, emphatically. "You swam as fast as you could. Why should you apologize for that? Weren't you tired when you were done? Or were you loafing throughout the swim?"

"Certainly not," said Ashley. "I was dead tired. I was trying the whole time. But Christopher is faster than me."

"OK," said Eddie. "But isn't one swimmer always going to be faster than the other? Or stronger? Or able to hold their breath longer? You wouldn't expect every frog to be exactly matched as swimmers, would you?"

Ashley answered hesitantly, "No. I guess not."

"Of course not. So why do you think we make all of our new trainees go through the Challenges? Is it just to humiliate half or more of our new recruits? Show them they can't swim as fast as someone else?"

"No. I don't think that's it," said Ashley. "Everyone has been too friendly around here. I don't think you would intentionally embarrass us."

"Exactly," said Eddie. "The Challenges are not about finding fast swimmers. So what do you think they *are* about?"

"Cooperative swimmers," Christopher blurted out. "Teammates. Frogs who truly adjust how fast they swim. Or what style they use. So their partner doesn't feel like they aren't contributing. Like they aren't good enough."

All three sat silent for a moment and let Christopher's words sink in. Eddie just smiled and waited for the other two to speak.

"Ashley, I'm sorry. I think what Eddie is trying to tell us must be right. You don't have to apologize to me. You were trying every bit as hard as I was. Why should you apologize to me?"

"Well, I don't know," said Ashley. "I hear what he's saying. But it still makes sense to me that you should get most of the credit for how we did today. You were the leader the whole way."

"Umm. Can I bring that up, now that we're on dry land and not gasping for air? I was wondering if I could ask you a question about the swim today."

"Sure," said Ashley. "Anything you want." Then hesitantly, "Is it OK if I ask you a question too?"

"Of course," said Christopher.

Eddie just sat and suddenly became very interested in the food on his plate.

"How come you didn't take the lead today, during the backstroke? I noticed as soon as we started that third leg you were very good at the backstroke. I was really struggling. How come you didn't go out ahead of me and pull me along a little?"

"Pull you along? I didn't want to break the rope. You saw how frayed it was after the first half of the swim."

"Sure, it showed some wear. But I think it would have handled a steady pull, just like it did during the first two legs."

"Maybe. But my question is, why did you pull so hard during the rest of the swim?"

"Hard? I didn't think I was pulling hard. I was just trying to help the team along. Didn't you think it made us faster to have me go out front and tug you along a little bit?"

"A little bit? Did you see my face go underwater at least a jillion times?"

"Uh? What do you mean?"

"I was almost drowning. I needed air. Why didn't you slow down?"

"Air? I didn't know you needed air. Why didn't you stop me and say something? We could have tread water any time you wanted. I actually could have used the break a few times."

"Well, why didn't you stop?"

"Because I was leading and swimming and I didn't see you needed air!"

"Well, I did! And clearly you wanted to lead, so I didn't take over during the backstroke. I just kept the rope slack. It was because of me that at least the rope didn't break."

"Yes, you did all you could to protect the rope, but didn't you think that maybe that also got in the way sometimes? It would have helped if you had been out front for awhile. And I still don't get why you didn't stop me and ask for a chance to catch your breath. Why didn't you tell me your face was going underwater?"

"Because what good would it have done?"

"Plenty! I wasn't trying to drown you!"

"Well, you nearly did!"

At this point, Eddie's face came up and he reached out both hands, as if to stop both of them from talking. "All right, both of you. I think I need to step in at this point. It seems you both finally got to say some things. Am I right about that?"

"Yes," said Christopher. "I still don't get why she didn't just speak up?"

"Yes," said Ashley. "How could he not know I was having trouble with air?"

Eddie looked calm, spoke more slowly than usual, and made frequent eye contact with both of them as he talked for the next couple of minutes.

"It's because you are different kinds of frogs. You have different personalities, and you do things differently. Which is OK. We have lots of different kinds of frogs here, and we're stronger for it. Everyone sees things differently. Everyone brings different kinds of problem solving abilities and experiences to our colony, and we love the diversity of our frogs. But it does make working together very difficult, especially at first.

"Ashley, you really like to value the relationship and you try to avoid conflict at all costs. We call that a passive style, and it is neither good nor bad. It's just what you bring to the pond with you, by default. Christopher, you have a more aggressive style. You naturally lead, you are very concerned with the task, and by default you expect that every other frog has the same style and priorities as you. But they don't.

"Learning to swim together starts off by recognizing that every frog is different from us. Every frog. Sometimes a lot different. Maybe occasionally we work with someone who is like us. But usually our own style needs to be managed – adapted – if we are going to swim the best we can as a team.

"We have a style here in the colony we call 'assertive.' It's a style of swimming, but it's also a way of communicating, a way of team problem solving. It is somewhere between passive and aggressive styles. When frogs are assertive, they respect the rights and talents and opinions of other frogs, something I think you could work on, Christopher. They also assert their own rights, talents and opinions – in an equal manner. They don't presume that their opinions or talents are any less important than anyone else's. This is something I think you could work on, Ashley.

"When both frogs are being assertive, they each get equal say in what the team does. They contribute their best thoughts and best ideas to the project. And they watch out for how they are being perceived by the other frog. In swimming, it means never completely ignoring what the other frog is experiencing, but it also means never being entirely passive, ignoring your own abilities and needs and allowing the other frog to do all of the work. I don't know if this is new to either of you, but have you heard about the assertive style before?"

Both shook their heads. Eddie asked them, "What do you think of it so far?"

"I think it makes perfect sense," Christopher said. "I really shouldn't just lead and make every decision during a team project, like the swim. I certainly don't want to make other frogs, like Ashley, *not* want to swim with me. But I probably need some help on what I can do differently. Being assertive, and not just taking the lead, is new to me."

"And I could use some help, too," said Ashley. "You're right. I could have spoken up more. Or used my body language, or something, to let Christopher know what I was feeling or when I thought

I could contribute more. But like Christopher said, this assertive style is new to me. Is there something we can do differently, specifically? How does one learn to be assertive?" Then she added, "And Christopher…thanks. I don't want to be mad at you. And I'm not. I may be a little bit mad at myself for not speaking up when I should have. I know we can swim together better if we get paired up again."

"Thanks, Ashley. I know we can too. I'll work on listening and watching you better."

Eddie smiled and went on, "Well, I'm glad you guys asked me about being assertive, but I'm afraid I've gone way past my lunch hour already. Why don't you both do what you did yesterday? Write down some lessons you want to remember, then share them with each other and talk them out. Maybe the best way to learn how to accommodate another frog's style is just to explain yourself to each other?"

Eddie got up, grabbed his tray, and as he walked out of the cafeteria, Ashley and Christopher eagerly thanked him for his time and got right to work. Luckily, there were plenty of dried lily pads in the napkin holder. They hurried to write down their thoughts before the next training session began.

After a few minutes, Ashley looked up and waited patiently for Christopher to finish. She had written three things, though she thought they were probably related.

The first was, "It takes courage to swim hard and tug on the rope, if you are not used to leading." Christopher agreed with her lesson. He had learned today that not everyone was as comfortable as he was at just diving in and leading. But he wanted to make sure Ashley understood why. In his opinion, each partner wasn't really helping the team swim faster if they weren't sometimes pulling on the rope. Pulling on the rope meant one frog was doing something different than the other frog, and perhaps better than the other frog.

Christopher finished, "Frogs just have to learn that pulling on the rope is sometimes a good thing. So I'd like to add a line below that lesson: 'Because pulling on the rope sometimes means you are helping the team.'"

Ashley agreed. "I'll have to work on that. I'll have to remember the rope can withstand a few tugs. Avoiding all possible conflict, all tugs on the rope, is not the best answer. I have to be willing to speak up."

"The lesson I wrote," added Christopher, "is: 'Watch and listen – make sure everyone is getting enough air.' I wanted to apologize to you again. I didn't notice what you were going through."

"No problem," Ashley said, dismissively.

"No, I'm serious," said Christopher. "This is something I know I need to work on. The real point of what I'm trying to say is … if the other frog is not getting enough air, or respect, stop and do something about it."

"I like that," Ashley said. "I'm going to add that last part below the lesson. 'If the other frog is not getting enough air, or respect, stop and do something about it.' For the projects and teamwork we are going to experience later in the colony, I think that will mean we will have to pay attention to how the other frog is reacting to our behavior."

"Yes, that is what I want to work on," said Christopher. "I think I sometimes get too caught up in winning or being fast or efficient. I may not be paying enough attention to my teammates."

"Well, each of us probably has to work on one of those two areas," Ashley said. "Either get better at focusing on the task, or get better at focusing on the relationships. Speaking of which, my next lesson is more about the former. I wrote, 'If you are not swimming hard, you are probably being dragged.' I confess, sometimes it felt like my effort just wasn't helping, particularly with Emma. So I may have let myself be dragged."

"I didn't feel that way," said Christopher.

"No, I don't think I did it with you," explained Ashley. "But I'm afraid if I don't learn to speak up, I may do it more. We have more Challenges. I really don't want to be an unproductive team member."

"I don't think you'll ever do that," Christopher added. "But I respect you want to work on that. Maybe we should add Eddie's line to this lesson – for both of us. 'If you're not swimming hard, you're probably being dragged AND just holding your breath until later.'"

Ashley gave a small laugh and agreed. "Yes, I probably hold my breath until later much too often. I'll have to learn to speak up when I first think things are going wrong. I don't want to be the kind of frog that complains to everyone else but never to the frog I'm mad at."

"Yeah, I can see how that would make it harder to be a good working colony, if some frogs were constantly being passive in their own teams, but complaining behind their teammates' backs. I confess, I don't usually have that problem. If anything, other frogs probably think I'm too upfront, maybe even rude, with my comments."

"Oh, I don't think so. But certainly no one has ever called me rude," said Ashley. "Maybe that's a sign that I'm not speaking up enough?"

"Well, I don't think you have to be rude just to speak up about your own feelings, needs, and opinions," said Christopher. "But, of course, if you never share that you disagree with frogs, that *is* probably a sign." He then added, "I do have one more lesson, if you have time. Though I think this probably only applies to me."

"Sure," said Ashley.

"I wrote down, 'If you are doing all of the pulling, is it your fault?' I know it doesn't apply to you, but it's something I think I need to ask myself."

"What do you mean, it doesn't apply to me? Of course it applies to me," said Ashley. "If I never ask to pull, isn't it just as much my fault as the other frog's?"

"Well, I don't know," Christopher said. "I certainly need to ask more often if the other frog has something to contribute."

"And I need to ask to lead, or take over some aspect of the swim, if I can," said Ashley. "That lesson definitely applies to me too."

"OK," said Christopher. "Go ahead and write it down if you want to."

"Well, how about if I make one small change," added Ashley. "What if we wrote it as: 'If only one of you is doing all of the pulling, is it your fault?' That makes it sound like it could apply to either passive or aggressive frogs. They both have to take responsibility for sharing the teamwork."

"Sounds even better," Christopher agreed. "I'm trying to work out how this lesson will apply once we get into the colony. I can imagine lots of situations where I'll have to be careful to listen to other frogs' ideas and not just do things the way I think they should be done."

"And I'll have to find a way to speak up," added Ashley. "Thinking back, I can remember lots of times at my old colony I probably should have spoken up more. But it's hard to change the way you've always done things."

"Yeah, that's for sure," added Christopher. "So, do you have any more?"

"Yes. I have one more," said Ashley. "'Always following or always leading is exhausting, and won't work well in the long run.' I added the second line so I would remember it might be OK in the short run, but eventually everyone should take a turn leading and following."

"Yeah, that makes perfect sense to me," said Christopher. "I definitely found leading exhausting, even though I guess it's my natural tendency."

"It's exhausting to follow, too," added Ashley. "I don't normally want to jump out in front, but I'm going to have to sometimes if my team is really going to do its best."

"Well, I'm glad we had another chance to talk," Christopher said. "*And* write down these lessons." He grabbed his tray and got up from the table.

Ashley quietly added, "I hope you don't mind that I said those things. They're really not something I usually bring up."

"No, of course not," said Christopher. "I much prefer getting things out in the open. And I needed to hear those things. I have to pay much better attention to my partner tomorrow."

"And I have to learn to speak up," said Ashley. "See you tomorrow morning?"

"You bet," Christopher said, and he turned down the hall toward his classroom.

As Ashley turned the other way, she realized she felt a little proud. She had never said those kinds of things to her co-workers at her last colony. But she should have. She decided to make herself a promise. Even if she didn't end up staying at GoodPondInc, and she had to go back to her old colony, she would try to remember these lessons and use them wherever she worked. But Ashley also felt a little bit of relief. She and Christopher had found a chance to talk things out. She really did want to be friends with him. She could tell the resentment she had felt toward him earlier had started to go away.

As Christopher walked down the hall, he was also glad they had talked. He now had a word he could apply to some of the frogs he had tried to work with in his old colony: "passive." He was certain this applied to at least a few of them and now he knew that it could be dealt with, if only he was willing to watch for it and adapt when necessary. But more importantly, he was glad he had talked with Ashley. He felt pretty confident he just had to make small adjustments to his style in order to accommodate other frogs. But he felt bad about the changes he thought she had to try. What must it be like to have to find courage? And to speak up when your first reaction is just to stay quiet? He couldn't imagine. But he knew if he got paired with Ashley again, he would do everything he could to help her out. He wanted to be friends with her, and he didn't want her to feel like swimming with him left her without any air. But he was worried for her. If she didn't learn to take the lead pretty quickly, like within the next couple of days, would GoodPondInc even keep her?

– Chapter Three –

On the third day, all of the frogs were familiar with the routine and waited patiently down by the pond's edge for Robert to begin his explanation. "Good morning," he began. "Everyone get a good breakfast?"

Most nodded in agreement and Robert gestured out toward the pond. "As you can see, we've set up four rows of lily pads out near the middle of the pond. What your tandem will do is swim out to the first set of pads, and swim under the entire length of the pads in one breath. When you come up for air, swim to the next set and swim under that row. Continue this pattern until you've swum under the last set. Then swim to shore."

"We know from experience that every one of you can hold your breath long enough to get under each of these sets, but it will be easier for some of you than others. As usual, you will be tied to a different frog today, so make sure you work together. Also, make sure you come out of the water together. As usual, the slowest teams will receive the lowest scores. Do you have any questions?"

No one spoke up. Ashley and Christopher were standing near each other. They were quietly talking and trying to sound confident about how well they were going to do today. As Robert read out the pairings, Christopher discovered he would be swimming with Emma and Ashley found out her partner was Buster.

"Don't worry about Emma," Ashley told Christopher. "She swims a lot like you, so I'm sure you two will get along fine."

"Same to you," Christopher said. "Buster swims more like you than me, so you should have an easy day today."

Christopher went off to tie his rope to Emma and approached

her with his hand out.

"Hi. I'm Christopher."

"Emma. Feeling strong today? I really need to do well. I think they might be ready to get rid of me if I don't place in the top half today. I didn't do so well the last two days."

"Well, me too. So I'm ready to go. I think I saw you swim with Ashley on the first day?"

"Was that her name? Nice frog, but it didn't go so well. She stopped me before we even got to the halfway point. We had to head to shore. It's funny. I think she can swim all right. But I'm not sure why she didn't want to swim with me. It's not like I was holding her back or anything. I was out front the whole time."

"Yeah. That's what she said. I just wanted to mention it because it shouldn't be a problem today. I've been out front on my team both days, so I think I can swim as fast as most frogs. So this should be fun. We might even win."

"Cool. I haven't even been in the top half. So you swim pretty strong? Want to go out in front sometimes? It's been tiring me out, pulling someone on every swim."

"No problem. I'll lead as much as you want. What do you say we try to split it up? You lead half the time and I'll lead the other?"

"OK. Sounds all right." But then she added, "As long as you are a really good swimmer, that is. I've got to finish in the top half, so maybe I'll have to pull more often … "

"OK. I hear you," Christopher replied. Then cautiously, "We'll see how it goes. At least we'll *plan* on you leading half the time and I'll lead half the time."

Robert was yelling out final instructions, so the crowd of frogs quieted down. He wanted to remind them that keeping the rope intact was important. But in case they hadn't noticed yet, the ropes were made out of lily pad stems, so they loved being in the water. If anyone's rope got stretched, they could always tread water for a little while and the rope would regain its shape and most of its strength. Robert again asked if anyone had any questions.

Emma and Christopher walked near the edge of the shore and stood next to Ashley and Buster, who were chatting away. Christopher felt good about the swim today. He was glad he had a strong swimmer as a partner, finally. Passive swimmers, he decided, were not his favorite kind of partners.

As Robert blew the whistle, all of the tandems headed into the water. As usual, it was no fun plunging through the weeds near shore, but quickly Emma and Christopher surged out front and were making good time toward the first row of lily pads.

Meanwhile, Ashley and Buster were figuring out their rhythm. They had decided to try and swim side-by-side since they both were tired of being dragged through the water. As the first row of lily pads approached, they found only five or six teams had arrived before them. They quickly nodded at each other, grabbed a big gulp of air, and plunged under the pads in near unison. As they swam forward, they discovered the passage beneath the pads was too narrow for them to swim side-by-side, so, after glancing at each other, Buster decided to go first and Ashley quickly followed. Since Ashley couldn't see where they were headed, she simply concentrated on keeping the rope slack while Buster swam as fast as he could. Only a couple of times did Ashley feel a tug on the rope. Each time, she noticed Buster adjusted his stroke and pretty soon they were making very good time under the pads. As they emerged, they saw they had caught up with the tandem ahead of them, so they stopped briefly to get some air.

Christopher and Emma emerged from the pads well ahead of Ashley and Buster, but still behind two tandems. Christopher had let Emma go ahead of him under the lily pads. As he caught up to Emma, he thought, well, at least I now know what Ashley has been going through. Though he had tried as hard as he could to keep the rope slack between them, Christopher had been kicked in the face by Emma several times. Each time, it threw him off of his stroke and slowed him down. And every time, Emma's next stroke would produce a big tug on the rope.

Christopher found this really annoying. It disrupted his swimming rhythm. He was particularly mad because he never noticed any change in Emma's swimming. He wondered how could she not know she was kicking him in the face? And why didn't she slow down when she felt the tug on her rope? Christopher didn't know, but he told himself to remember this feeling when it was his turn to lead. He knew he couldn't *guarantee* he wouldn't kick Emma, but at least he would remember to do something about it. Meanwhile, Emma swam on – apparently oblivious to Christopher. The only good thing, Christopher thought, was at least they were going fast. He was sure they would finish in the top half of the group, even if he was getting really frustrated with her.

As Christopher and Emma caught their breath, he could see they were catching the team ahead of them. But he noticed her strokes were starting to get a little wild. It could be she was getting tired, but he felt he was getting splashed a lot as Emma plowed through the water. He was sure his stroke wasn't splashing her nearly as much. As they approached the second row of lily pads, Christopher swam a little faster and got out in front. With a quick look back, he and Emma timed their breathing and they plunged under the pads without really changing their pace.

Ashley and Buster approached the second set of lily pads still swimming in a coordinated rhythm. They were side-by-side and neither seemed interested in going out ahead of the other. Just a few inches from the first pad, both of them stopped and started treading water, waiting for the other to give directions. Ashley spoke first, remembering it took courage to discuss things and to lead. She offered to go ahead of Buster this time. Buster agreed that would probably be best. He had had a hard time seeing in the dark under the lily pads, plus he had nearly run out of air. He said he hoped Ashley could swim faster than him because he wanted to get out from under the pads quicker than before. Ashley said she would sure try. They each grabbed a big gulp of air and dove under the lily pads.

As Ashley made her way under the pads, she felt really uncomfortable swimming ahead of Buster. She was trying to swim fast since Buster had wanted her to, but she was trying hard not to kick Buster in the face or tug on his rope. Unfortunately, she found this was nearly impossible to do all of the time. Since she was in front, she couldn't really tell where Buster was or how fast he was going every single second. But every time Ashley slowed down and looked back, Buster furiously waved at her to go on. He clearly wanted to get out from under the pads quickly and he seemed fine with Ashley leading, despite the occasional tug or kick.

As they came out from under the lily pads, Ashley quickly swam to the side in case another team came through and started to tread water. Buster popped up, gulped several times for air, and eventually smiled ear hole-to-ear hole as he thanked Ashley for the swim.

"That was good," Buster said, still gasping for air. "I think that row was longer than the first. It really helped that you pulled me along."

"But I'm sorry if I kicked you a couple of times," said Ashley.

"Oh, don't worry about it. I didn't mind that much. And really, you did what I asked you to do, so how can I complain?"

"OK," Ashley replied. "It feels weird to be out ahead of anyone but I'll do it again if you want me to."

Buster answered he thought maybe that would be best. But after that, he started talking about the last two Challenges. Ashley quietly listened and watched a pair of frogs emerge from the pads and swim past them.

Near the front of the pack, Christopher and Emma were making good time. They were now in second place and had just emerged from the third row of lily pads. Emma had been leader again after Christopher had taken his turn leading under the second row of pads. Both underwater swims had gone reasonably well. Each discovered that no matter who was leading, the one in the back occasionally got kicked or had their rope tugged. But since they were both so focused on the Challenge, neither seemed to mind too much.

As they came up on the last row of lily pads, Christopher found himself thinking, If only she wouldn't splash so much. That's probably just the way she swims, but it's still annoying. Christopher realized all of that splashing made it a bit harder for him to get the air he needed. As they dove under the last row of lily pads, Christopher took the lead and calculated they could catch the first place team if they swam really hard.

Back between lily pad rows two and three, Buster was still chatting. Ashley became convinced he didn't even notice there were no more frogs coming out from under the lily pads. It wasn't until Robert yelled at them from the shore that Buster seemed to realize they needed to go back to swimming. As Buster took off, Ashley dutifully followed and they quickly made it to lily pad row three. Ashley led under that row, and the next, and each time Buster emerged from under the lily pads short of breath, but not mad. Eventually, they walked out of the water and onto the beach. Their rope looked stretched, but it wasn't broken.

As they untied their rope, they noticed a few tandems had broken their ropes and were sitting apart from each other, not talking. But on the far side of the beach, a boisterous group of frogs were comparing stories about the Challenge. Ashley and Buster drifted off toward the loud group and noticed Christopher and Emma were in the middle, with big smiles.

"Hey, Ashley. How did you do?" asked Christopher.

"Not very well," said Ashley. "I think we came in last place."

"What? How did you do that?" Christopher said, looking sympathetic but also slightly in shock.

"I'm not sure. We just didn't have a good swim," replied Ashley. Buster didn't say anything. He was still very clearly mad at Christopher. "How well did you and Emma do?" Ashley asked.

"Uh. Well. We got first place," Christopher said, hesitating. "We put a lot of strain on the rope, but it held up. We were both really tired. I thought I was going to collapse at any moment. And I did have some trouble getting air sometimes, so I now know what you mean."

Buster just "hmphed" and walked away. Ashley congratulated Christopher and said she'd known they would do well together.

"How did you and Buster do so badly?" Christopher asked when Buster was out of earshot.

"Well, it probably was because we stopped and treaded water so long after the second row of lily pads. I could see a lot of other frogs were passing us, but he said he needed to catch some air, and I didn't know how to tell him 'let's get going again.'"

"Oh, I was afraid of that," said Christopher. "Buster doesn't put in a lot of effort. And you didn't want to be the bad guy and tell him he was doing something wrong."

"He wasn't doing anything wrong," Ashley offered. "He just took too much time to chat."

"That's what I mean," said Christopher. "Maybe Emma and I swam too hard and didn't really give ourselves a chance to rest at all. But the other situation is just as bad. Stopping to tread water and just chatting can be a real problem if you are supposed to be swimming forward – if you are supposed to be getting something done."

"Well," Ashley hesitated. "I don't know. Maybe you're right. But it probably won't matter now," she added, sadly. "I think we ended up last, so I'll probably not make the program anyway."

"Oh, don't be such a worry wart," said Christopher with a big smile. He knew Ashley would get the old joke about warts, since frogs didn't have them and toads did. "There might have been teams that couldn't even make it under the lily pads. You know some of the rows were longer than the others. At least you finished. I did see a bunch of frogs with broken ropes."

"Maybe," said Ashley, trying to smile. "But I wish I had spoken up. I knew we were wasting a lot of time. I don't know what's wrong with me? I'm just so afraid of getting another frog mad at me."

As they turned and headed toward the showers, both Christopher and Ashley saw Robert pull a few of the frogs aside and lead them toward the main building. They had not seen him do this before. They quickly talked about how maybe the colony had made some decisions about who to let go. Christopher said some of the frogs going with Robert had broken their ropes on every swim. But Ashley pointed out that at least two of the frogs she recognized had never broken their ropes, at least not that she could remember. She said breaking the rope must not be the only reason Robert had taken some of the frogs up the hill. They promised each other they would find out what they could during their morning training session and share notes at lunch.

Christopher seemed unconcerned as he walked off toward the men's showers. But Ashley admitted to herself she was very worried. What if she got pulled aside tomorrow? Buster and she were certainly the last group out of the water today. What did she need to do differently tomorrow?

At lunch, Ashley and Christopher both confirmed that the frogs walking with Robert were no longer with the colony. It appeared the Challenges were for real. How you swam with another frog *did* make a difference in whether GoodPondInc wanted you to work here.

After quickly eating, Ashley said she was eager to hear what Christopher had learned on his swim that morning. She said she was worried her performance was going to get her kicked out of the colony.

"You stress about it too much," Christopher reassured her. "You've been doing very well at keeping the rope healthy, and I still think most of those frogs had broken their ropes every morning.

You didn't even break yours once, so I think you're in good shape. But I'm eager to talk too. I wrote down a couple of lessons already. I think I learned a lot swimming with Emma. For example, my first lesson today was 'No one wants to get kicked in the face. It's better to swim side-by-side.'"

"Oh, that's a good one," said Ashley. "I can tell you, swimming with Emma, and being dragged and kicked most of the way, was very un-fun. Buster and I swam side-by-side this morning as much as we could. I know it made me feel better knowing he wasn't behind me and I wasn't kicking him in the face."

"You mean, there was a time you kicked him?" asked Christopher, almost unbelieving.

"Yes. Whenever we went under the lily pads, I had to lead. He said he wasn't very good at holding his breath, so he wanted me to swim faster and pull him along. I guess it worked pretty well. He wasn't mad even though there were times I tugged on his rope or accidentally kicked him."

"That's terrific," Christopher said. "I'm glad you finally got a chance to lead. You know, it's really OK if someone follows you once in a while, even if they find it uncomfortable some of the time."

"Yes," she replied, "it felt very awkward. But I did learn something from it. The first lesson I wrote today was, 'Some tugs and splashes will just happen.' Even though I was really frustrated getting splashed by Emma, when I swam with you and Buster I realized it was never intentional. If two frogs have to swim together, of course there will be some splashes and tugs."

"Right," Christopher said. "It is tandem swimming after all."

"Great line," Ashley said. "Let's add that below the first part. 'Some tugs and splashes will just happen. It *is* tandem swimming after all.'"

"I like that," Christopher said, "and I agree one hundred percent. If you're going to work with someone that close, for that long, there are going to be some tugs and splashes, and maybe even accidental kicks in the face. But both frogs are likely to do it to each other at different points. I say ignore the splashes and tugs when you can and just keep swimming, with a good attitude, if at all possible."

"Well, that's the challenge, right?" added Ashley. "I'm sure when we get to work in the colony, we'll get offended at something someone else says or does. That's bound to happen sometimes. Particularly if we work alongside each other this close. But not getting mad about it – letting it roll off our backs, is pretty hard. I know. I've worked a lot longer than you have. Fifteen years in another colony."

"Fifteen! I never would have guessed," said Christopher. "So, do frogs offend other frogs a lot of the time?"

"No, that's not what I'm saying," answered Ashley. "I'm not trying to say that frogs try to offend each other, but … there are so many interactions, so many things that get said and done near or to each other when you are working really closely with another frog that inevitably one of them doesn't take something the right way. I think my point is to remember this lesson. Sometimes splashes and tugs just happen. Try to ignore them if you can. Keep a good attitude and try to work through it. Don't break the rope."

"Yeah," Christopher said. "Back to rule number one: don't break the rope. Keep the relationship intact."

"But, I'm having trouble with my next lesson," Ashley said. "Did you and Emma ever tread water during your swim?"

"Yeah, a little," said Christopher. "We probably should have a bit more. I think we'd have been more careful about not splashing or bumping each other if we'd stopped occasionally and just treaded water."

"Well, that's kind of what I'm trying to say with my second lesson," Ashley continued. "I wrote 'It's OK to tread water for a while – it helps the rope and it allows everyone time to get air if they need it.' I treaded water a couple of times the other mornings, but when Buster and I did it this morning, it was terrible. We did it for way too long."

"I see," said Christopher. "So you want to add a line to that lesson somehow. Treading water is OK some of the time, but you can do it too much."

"Yes. I guess that's what I'm thinking."

"OK," Christopher said. "So how about adding a line like 'But remember – it's not really the same as swimming toward a goal.' Does that seem to capture the right thought?"

"Perfect," Ashley said. "I'm worried that it could be a tight fence to walk. How do you know when you're appropriately hanging out with a co-worker, building a relationship – versus when you're doing it too much? I certainly don't want it to get in the way of doing whatever I or we are supposed to accomplish."

"Well, that lesson seems like it should be addressed to me, then," Christopher said. "I probably didn't tread water enough the first two days when I swam with you and Buster. I can tell he's still mad at me. Of course, with Emma, it didn't seem to matter that much. She's more like me."

"Yes, that seems to be the problem," Ashley added. "Some frogs apparently just naturally like to put their nose to the grindstone and get to work, and others prefer to enjoy each other's company. I don't want to think that either is wrong, but it does mean having to maybe speak up or change what I do for different frogs."

"Yup, you have to change what you do to match different frogs," Christopher added emphatically.

"Oh well. I'm sure that will come up again. Did you have another lesson?" asked Ashley.

"One more. I was thinking of my first two swims when I wrote this. It kind of follows up on what I just said about Buster. 'Tandem swims require a lot of patience.' And then I added, 'but at least you arrive together.'"

"That's a great lesson," Ashley commented. She added with a smile, "I didn't think patience was something you aggressive types were very fond of."

"No, clearly not," said Christopher, going along with the joke and smiling back. "But I guess that's why we need to work on it. I think if I ever swim with Buster again, I'm going to have to really work on slowing down, going at a pace he's comfortable with. Or we will just break our rope again."

"So, your lesson, 'Tandem swims require a lot of patience, but at least you arrive together,' is meant to remind you to work on yourself, and be patient whenever you have to be in a team environment?"

"Exactly," Christopher replied. "I'm learning not everyone is as all-fired-up to get done as I am, all of the time. But I can't change them on every occasion, so I'm going to have to learn to deal with them. I'm going to have to remember to be patient. And to value the rope – the relationship – just as much as I value getting the task done."

Ashley said she agreed with that, but perhaps her personal issues were different. As she looked at the clock, she remarked on how late it was getting and she and Christopher started cleaning up their trays. Before they could leave, Eddie came over.

"Hi, Ashley. Christopher. Was the Challenge this morning about swimming under the lily pads? How did it go?"

"Not too bad," Ashley replied. "Turns out my partner was having trouble holding his breath under the long rows, so I pulled him a little bit on the underwater swims. He didn't seem to mind and it just seemed to make sense. Plus, there was no way two frogs could swim through there side-by-side. There just wasn't enough room."

"So, how did you feel about pulling someone through the water? Didn't you say you resented that when it happened to you?" asked Eddie.

"Yes, but this was different," explained Ashley. "First, he seemed to want me to do it. And we wouldn't have made such good time if I hadn't pulled him at least a little. And it wasn't like it made it harder for him to breathe. His face was underwater anyway."

"Yes, but couldn't pulling on the rope help even if you were both above water?" asked Eddie.

"Sure it could, Ashley," interrupted Christopher. "It helped my team. There were many times I pulled on someone's rope. I'm sure we went faster because of it. Those were the times I was helping the slower swimmer swim faster."

"Yes, but some of those times, frogs had trouble getting air," explained Ashley.

"OK," Christopher said. "So, you're saying if they didn't have trouble getting air it would have been all right?"

"Umm. Yes, I guess so," Ashley said. "*And* if they gave you permission."

"You both are right," Eddie said. "It's been my experience working here that sometimes one frog has to lead. One frog may have to make decisions or direct the conversation. And it is not always a bad thing. Maybe they are better at some part of the process, like you were the stronger swimmer underwater, Ashley. Other times it might be because the situation simply demands that you go one at a time, as in the narrow passage under the lily pads. But either way, there are many times when one frog has to lead."

Christopher and Ashley said they understood. They agreed to add another lesson to their dried lily pad: 'It's OK to let one swimmer lead for a while.'

But Christopher worried that some swimmers seemed to really enjoy letting the other swimmer lead. Perhaps they were using that as a way to get out of the extra work required to lead. He excused Ashley from this, of course. He was thinking of Buster and their first swim.

"You might be right," Ashley said. "So let's add one more line to that lesson. 'It's OK to let one swimmer lead for a while. But help out as much as you can.' No one really wants to drag another frog through the water, so if you aren't the frog leading, help out as much as you can."

"Sounds good," Eddie added. "By the way, did you hear some frogs got asked to go home today?"

"Yeah," Christopher said. "Is that kind of thing going to continue?"

"Yes, tomorrow is also a frog elimination day," Eddie said. "But don't be nervous. When I hear you both talk, I can tell you are understanding what it really means to be a good team member. Just remember your lessons on your swim tomorrow."

"Of course," Ashley added.

"Sure," Christopher said.

But both of them got suddenly quiet. They were so consumed with their thoughts that they forgot to say goodbye to Eddie as he left.

Eventually, as they walked out of the cafeteria together, they tried to say reassuring things to each other. Ashley congratulated Christopher on his first place finish. And he said there was no way the colony would get rid of such an accommodating frog as her. But neither really believed the other. Real nervousness was starting to set in now that some of the frogs had actually been eliminated. Would they make it through tomorrow?

– Chapter Four –

As Ashley headed down to the pond for the fourth Challenge, she admitted to herself she was more nervous than before. She was certain her bad performance on day three had put her near the bottom of the list. If she didn't do well today, she felt pretty sure they would ask her to leave.

When the group gathered for Robert's instructions, she saw Christopher and Emma still re-telling the story of how they had won the third day's Challenge. She was surprised to find she was disappointed she couldn't talk to Christopher alone, but she was happy he seemed to be popular. Robert's announcements interrupted her train of thought.

"Today, as you may have noticed, we are down several frogs. The colony puts a great deal of importance on the Challenges, and if frogs can't learn to tandem swim, then we believe they will have a hard time adjusting to our team-oriented culture. However, I don't want any of you to panic. It won't help your swim today. If you let your emotions get the best of you, you won't collaborate very well. So try to relax.

"However, I do want to emphasize that word 'collaborate.' The fourth Challenge will be to swim to the two sets of lily pads you see out in the pond. But this time, you will be tied to a different frog for each part of the swim. This means you will have to get up on the lily pads and tie your rope to a new frog. To make it easy to keep track of which frog is your next partner, each tandem will be assigned another tandem as their partners. Therefore, you will start with your own teammate, switch to one of the frogs on your partner team at the first lily pad, switch to the other partner on the next lily pad, and swim to shore with this third partner. Does anyone have any questions before we begin?"

"Yes," said Emma. "What if we are way ahead of the other team? Are we supposed to just sit there and wait for them to catch up?"

"Definitely," said Robert. "In fact, you have to wait for them at every checkpoint, including the end. All four teammates have to emerge from the water at the same time in order for the Challenge to be completed correctly. Are there any other questions?"

Nobody said a word and Robert started calling out names. Fear was starting to creep onto the faces of many, if not most of the frogs. For the first time, they all knew this was an elimination day. And what was obvious was that each frog's chances of doing well depended not just upon one other frog, but *three* other frogs. If you were anything but the strongest or the weakest swimmer in the bunch, at least part of the time you were going to pull and get pulled. Ashley was getting more nervous by the minute.

As the names were read out, Christopher was disappointed he did not get paired with Ashley. She wasn't even on his paired team. However, he was glad that she got Emma on her paired team. He knew Emma could at least pull her faster for a third of the race – faster than she could probably swim for herself. He was not happy with his luck, however. He got Buster on his paired team. They had broken the rope on the first day and he knew from Ashley's story that Buster didn't mind treading water and chatting if he got the chance. Christopher was afraid he would really slow him down.

Christopher's first partner was a frog he didn't know very well named Devon. Christopher had noticed he was pretty quiet most of the time, but he always seemed to finish near the front of the pack. Buster's partner, and Christopher's third teammate, was called Brit, short for Brittany. She was known as a talker throughout the group and immediately Christopher feared he and Devon would be waiting a long time at the first lily pad if Buster and Brittany decided to stop and chat.

Ashley felt a bit better knowing Emma was going to be one of her partners. Her first partner turned out to be a frog named Andrew and Emma's first partner was a frog named Jennifer. Both of them had finished near the back of the pack each day and neither was known for being a very good partner. In fact, Andrew was best known for throwing a fit on the first day when his partner refused to swim the style he wanted. Rumor had it he had intentionally broken his rope and swum toward shore. Fortunately for him, Andrew had been paired with rather passive swimmers the following two days and he had made it past the first frog elimination day. Ashley had also heard that Jennifer as one of the laziest frogs in the group. Each frog she had swum with complained there were times she simply went limp and let them drag her through the water. Ashley wasn't excited about today's swim at all. Now she was positive she wouldn't make it to lunch.

When Robert's whistle blew, Ashley and Andrew started to make their way to the water. But within a few feet of shore, Andrew suddenly stopped. Ashley was just getting ready to plunge in and the sudden yank on her rope made her fall backward. She looked up angrily, but before she could shout anything, she noticed Andrew looked frightened.

"What's going on?" she asked.

"Nothing!" Andrew angrily replied. "Just give me a minute."

"OK," she answered. She watched as Andrew seemed to be talking himself into something. She couldn't hear what he was saying, but she knew it had something to do with the weeds because he kept looking up at them, nervously. Shortly, he started to walk slowly toward the water and she followed.

"Are you ready?" she asked.

"Of course!" he shouted back. "What do you think I am? A tadpole? I'll go first, since you can't seem to make up your mind." He started toward the weeds very slowly. Ashley didn't know what to do, so she just followed quietly. She knew they had to get swimming pretty quickly. She could see most of the tandems were already out of the weeds and into open water.

As they gradually made it out of the weeds, Ashley could tell Andrew's confidence was growing. He started to swim stronger and eventually started pulling on Ashley's rope. It dawned on her she should stop and mention the rope to him, but his weird behavior at the shore made her decide to stay quiet. She had never met a frog that seemed so afraid of weeds. But they were catching up to the other tandems at this pace and she decided it was best to just keep the rope as slack as she could.

As Christopher and Devon got into water over their heads, Christopher was surprised to discover Devon seemed to prefer the sidestroke. This was a peculiar swimming style for frogs, since it used a scissors kick and a weird, asymmetrical hand stroke with the upper body. All the frogs Christopher had ever known preferred the crawl or the breast stroke. It took him a while to adjust to Devon's rhythm. It wasn't long, however, before he realized Devon was actually matching Christopher's timing and rhythm. Though the rope between them was short, and they should be getting in each other's way, they were actually swimming pretty smoothly. And even though they were swimming different strokes, Christopher found that Devon had a knack for stroking and kicking in such a way he rarely ever had an impact on Christopher's swimming. Soon, Christopher stopped worrying about it and just swam as fast as he could. When they reached the first lily pad, they were in front of nearly everyone, and Christopher realized Devon had never pulled on his rope. Breathlessly, they climbed up on the lily pad, untied their rope and waited. They had no idea how long it would be before Buster and Brit arrived.

When Ashley and Andrew arrived at the first lily pad, Emma and Jennifer were waiting for them. Ashley was completely worn out because Andrew had essentially dragged her through the water. As she got out of the water, she could tell Emma was not in a good mood either. She seemed unusually tired for such a strong swimmer. Ashley didn't want to start a possible conversation, so she quietly untied her rope and tied herself to Jennifer. Emma tied the other end of her rope to Andrew and the two of them dove into the water.

As Ashley got ready to jump, she heard Jennifer say, "You had better be a strong swimmer." Ashley stopped and looked at Jennifer. "I can't pull anyone," Jennifer said. "I'm just not built that way." Ashley replied she thought she was a pretty strong swimmer, and maybe they could just keep up with each other. Ashley explained she didn't really like pulling on the rope, and sometimes it didn't even seem to help. Jennifer just shrugged and jumped feet first in to the water. Ashley's rope yanked and she had to jump into the water after Jennifer, barely missing her.

As Ashley began swimming toward the second lily pad, she noticed Jennifer indeed was a slow swimmer. Though she seemed to be going through the motions, it was apparent Ashley could swim much faster. She had to decide pretty quickly if she was going to pull or drag Jennifer through the water. Fortunately, they didn't seem to be losing ground relative to many of the other frog teams. Some were treading water, arguing about what stroke to do, what direction to take, or just who would get in front. Ashley decided her best approach would be to compromise. She would pull on the rope sometimes and, other times, she would just slow down and swim next to Jennifer. Maybe if she were swimming beside Jennifer and not in front of her, she wouldn't just give up and let Ashley do all of the work. As they progressed toward the second lily pad, Ashley decided her approach seemed to be working. Ashley was not getting tired and was actually recovering somewhat while swimming next to Jennifer. Every now and then, Ashley would go out ahead and pull on Jennifer a little, speeding them up for a little while. But each time she slowed down to swim beside her, Jennifer would surprisingly thank Ashley for her help. It did seem to Ashley that Jennifer was at least very kind and considerate. But she definitely wasn't trying very hard.

When they arrived at the pad, Ashley finally had a chance to ask Jennifer a few questions. They had a little while to wait because it was obvious Emma and Andrew were making terrible time. They seemed to be arguing over every detail of the swim. Ashley asked Jennifer why she seemed so unconcerned about not finishing quickly. Wasn't she worried that finishing near the back would make the colony ask her to leave? Jennifer replied she wasn't really worried. Her father had told her that most colonies would keep at least eight frogs from each new recruiting class, so she only had to be no lower than eighth. She figured she had finished eighth, on average, each day, so things were working out OK. Ashley said she had not heard this, but wouldn't it still be better to see how high up she could finish? Wasn't she at least going to try and do her best? Jennifer replied "Why bother? I'll get the same job and the same pay no matter where I finish. Why try so hard?"

When Buster and Brit arrived at the first lily pad they were clearly at the back of the pack. Christopher was sure they had stopped and talked a while, maybe many times. Christopher quickly tied his rope to Buster and watched as Brit and Devon jumped into the water. Before Buster jumped, however, Christopher stopped and asked if they could talk quickly. "Sure," Buster replied, guardedly.

"First," Christopher said, "I wanted to apologize for what I did on the first day. I realize now I was swimming too hard and not being considerate of how you were doing on the swim. I wish we hadn't broken the rope and I want this swim to go well, for both of us."

"Thanks," Buster said. "I wish we hadn't broken the rope also. But, I was trying to let you know I couldn't go that fast. You didn't even seem to notice I was going underwater. And I pulled on the rope at least a dozen times … "

"Yes, I realize that now," Christopher said. "But I didn't realize it then. I thought I was helping the team by swimming as fast as I could and pulling you along through the water. This swimming with another frog is really new to me, and I'm beginning to see how important it is to keep the rope intact, and to pay attention to your partner. "

"Well, thanks, I guess," Buster said. "I want to do well, too. But I don't want to do it in a way that makes my partner annoyed."

"OK," Christopher said. "So, why don't we agree I'll go slower at first, and if you can keep up and don't mind how I'm swimming, I'll gradually speed up. If you don't like it, just let me know somehow and we'll adjust to each other. If we're halfway there and you can put up with it, I'll try to pull on the rope some just to see if we can finish a bit faster. Does that sound all right?"

"Umm. OK," Buster said. "I really don't like my rope being pulled, but if you're willing to let me slow you down sometimes, I'll give it a try."

"Great. Well, let's go," Christopher said. "I know we'd both like to finish this quickly today."

When Emma and Andrew finally arrived at the second lily pad, Ashley was fully rested and eager to get going. She saw Emma untie her rope from Andrew and could tell it was badly frayed and stretched. It was obvious their swim had not gone well. She offered the free end of her rope to Emma and they quickly got back in the water. Meanwhile, over her shoulder, she heard Jennifer make the same comment to Andrew – she was saying she hoped he was a strong swimmer. Ashley didn't wait to hear his answer.

As Ashley and Emma started to swim, it was obvious Emma wanted to make up for lost time. She was chugging along in her usual splashy, noisy style, but Ashley didn't mind. Maybe because Emma was tired from her earlier swims, Ashley found it rather easy to keep up with her. Pretty quickly, they both discovered their feet could touch bottom. They stopped right at the water's edge and looked back, expecting to see Andrew and Jennifer right behind. They were surprised when Andrew came out of the water a short time later. He went right beside them and stalked right onto shore. His rope had clearly been cut or broken, and he didn't say a word to anyone. He had an angry look on his face and he headed straight for the showers. Ashley's heart sank. Clearly, this meant her time at the colony was going to end.

Emma turned to Ashley and asked what they should do. "I'm not sure," Ashley replied. "Obviously we're not going to come out of the water with all four of us. I guess we should at least wait for Jennifer."

"I don't know," Emma said. "I really didn't enjoy swimming with her. She made me drag her almost the whole way. If we at least get out of the water now we can finish in the top half of the group. Who knows when she's going to show up?"

"I know," Ashley said. "She's definitely not motivated to swim as fast as she can. But I think if the goal of the Challenge is to come out of the water as a complete team, we should at least wait for as many members of our team as we can. Plus, we don't know when she's going to arrive. It *might* be soon."

"I'll be surprised if she isn't the last one here," said Emma. "But I guess you're right. If you want to stay, I'll stay here with you. I don't want to leave you by yourself."

"Thanks," Ashley said. "I don't know if I'm right, but I'm glad we're going to wait this out together."

And they waited. It turned out to be quite a while.

When Christopher and Buster reached the second lily pad, he found Devon and Brit had arrived just ahead of them. He was surprised. He and Buster had passed quite a few swimmers and he figured Brit would really slow Devon down. But Christopher was grateful they had made up some lost ground and he certainly didn't want to question his good luck. As he tied his rope to Brit, he thanked Buster for the swim they had just completed.

"No. Thank you," Buster said. "I was really afraid you were going to do the same thing you did the first day, but you were much better today. And I'm really glad you let me stop and tread water that one time. I can't tell you how much I needed that."

"Well, no problem," Christopher said. "I think you did great. Look at how many tandems we passed. I hope I didn't pull on your rope too hard during that last part of the swim."

"No, that was OK since I knew it was coming," Buster said. "I knew you would stop if I needed you to, so it seemed all right. And it did make me faster." Turning to Devon he added, "You ready? I think we can really get out front of some of these frogs if we get in the water fast."

"Sure," said Devon. They jumped in the water and Christopher and Brit jumped in close behind.

After a few strokes in the water, Christopher remembered to check on Brit and lifted his head a little. He was surprised to find Brit was doing a poor imitation of Devon's sidestroke. Her head was above water and her arms were making the right motions, but she seemed to have trouble with the scissors kick. Christopher slowed down and got close enough to shout over to Brit.

"Hey, I never saw you do the sidestroke before?"

"Yeah, Devon taught it to me," Brit said.

"Really? That is the stroke he uses. But why are you trying a new stroke during the Challenges? Aren't you afraid you'll be too slow?"

"Maybe," Brit said. "But it seems to work well for me. I think Devon uses it because he can keep an eye on his partner the whole time and change how he swims. But I like it because I can keep my head above water. Maybe talk a little while I'm swimming."

"Yeah. I guess it's good for that too," Christopher said. Then a thought struck him. "Hey, why don't we swim a little bit like I did with Buster? I'll go out ahead and pull on your rope just a little to try and speed us up occasionally, but after a while I'll come back and swim with you. I'll try this sidestroke with you and we can talk while we keep swimming. How does that sound?"

"OK. I guess we can try it," Brit said. "I'm not real fond of having my rope pulled, but I can probably put up with it for a little while. Will you come back and swim with me if I give a big yank on the rope?"

"Sure," Christopher said. He was thinking what did he have to lose? At least this way they would be going fast some of the time. It was probably the best he could do with a talker like Brit.

When Christopher and Brit finally made it to shore, they found Devon and Buster waiting for them. Somehow, again, Devon had made good time with his partner. The four of them walked out of the water together and headed straight for Robert. A quick scan of the beach convinced Christopher they had finished somewhere near the middle of the pack. As he looked for Ashley, his eyes came up empty. Eventually, he turned back to the water and saw her sitting in the shallow water with Emma. He wondered what could have possibly happened to her tandem team. It looked to him like she was just going to sit there and wait until everyone had come out of the water. For her sake, he was nervous. He didn't want her to be last!

As the morning wore on, Ashley and Emma just sat. For both of them, it seemed like an eternity. One by one, the other teams emerged from the water. Eventually, when it seemed like there couldn't be any team left to finish, Jennifer swam into view and slowly emerged from the water. Ashley and Emma walked out right beside her.

Ashley quickly realized all of the other teams had gone to the showers. Only Robert and Christopher were waiting on the shore. She was certain she, Emma, and Jennifer would immediately be escorted to the main building by Robert. But he didn't say a thing. He just made more notes on his pad, told them to hit the showers, and then he started off toward the main building.

Christopher weakly congratulated them for finishing and walked toward the showers with Ashley. Emma was staring blankly at the ground, not believing how her fortunes had changed in just one day – from first to last. Ashley tried to sound positive and told her not to worry. Jennifer, meanwhile, was fuming. As soon as Robert was out of hearing, she started talking about how Andrew had been im-possible to swim with. Even before they had gotten in the water, he had tried to tell her how she was supposed to swim. They were only in the water a few strokes before he was just pulling her through the water, against her will. She told him to slow down and she even threatened to tell Robert how he was treating her, but suddenly he lost his cool. She wasn't really that surprised when he intentionally broke the rope and started swimming toward shore. "If he hadn't done it," she said, "I probably would have anyway."

She went on to explain that when it happened, she didn't know what to do, so she just treaded water for a while. Eventually, she decided she could at least make it to shore. She was grateful Ashley and Emma had waited for her. But Ashley noticed that at no time did Jennifer actually apologize to them. Clearly, Ashley thought, she must have realized her wait had affected their scores as well. Ashley decided not to confront Jennifer, but hoped she wouldn't have to swim with her again. She thought perhaps nothing was ever going to make Jennifer work hard. But more importantly, Ashley worried that this would be her last day at GoodPondInc.

At lunch, Christopher found Emma and sat beside her. He realized too late that Andrew was also sitting at the table. He had to sit between them.

"So, how's it going guys?" Christopher asked. He was really hoping only Emma would answer.

"Not good," said Andrew. "In fact, really, really bad. I have to see Robert right after lunch, and I know what that means. I'm probably out of here."

"Oh, that's not for sure," said Emma, but Christopher felt the odds were pretty good.

"Can you believe that Jennifer?" Andrew asked. "She tried to get me to agree to pull her even before we jumped in the water! What was that all about? And sure enough, as soon as we got in the water she turned into dead weight. I've never had to work so hard with someone so lazy. She can swim. She just doesn't want to. It's not fair. Why should I have to go and she gets to stay?"

"Umm. I'm not sure she's going to," Ashley said as she joined their table.

"What?" Christopher said. "You heard something about Jennifer?"

"Yeah," Ashley said. "I heard her say she has to go see Robert right after lunch. My guess is we came out of the water so late Robert couldn't gather up all of the frogs he wanted to talk to, so he is waiting until after lunch to let them know whether they are staying or leaving GoodPondInc."

"Great!" Andrew exclaimed. "I knew that was going to happen. Well, at least Jennifer is going to be called on the rug too. If I have to go, I want her to have to go, as well."

Realizing Andrew was called to the office as well, Ashley tried to backtrack. "I don't know that is actually why she was called there," said Ashley. "It was just something I heard. You know how wrong rumors can be."

"We'll see," said Andrew. "I don't think I want to be here anyway. This place is nothing like the colony I came from."

"Mine either," said Emma. "What's with all of this tandem swimming stuff anyway? Where I come from, you work hard, you're better than everybody else, and you get ahead. Why should I have to be tied to another frog? It's stupid!"

"Umm. It is a bit different," said Christopher, not wanting to get her madder. "But I understand that's the way they do things in this colony, even after we're done with the Challenges. They do a lot of teamwork. I guess they want us to be ready for that."

"Ready for it?" said Emma. "I don't even think I want to do it." And she got up from the table, grabbed her tray, and walked away.

"Yeah, who would want to work like that?" said Andrew, and he got up and left.

Pretty soon, Ashley and Christopher were by themselves. He finally broke the silence. "I'm sorry you finished last this morning, Ashley. I know it wasn't really your fault. Jennifer and Andrew were the worst possible frogs you could have been paired with."

"No, that's OK," Ashley said. "I'm sure Buster and Brit were no picnic. But you seemed to do OK with them. How did you manage to finish so well when you can swim so much faster than either of them?"

"I think it was because I talked to them," Christopher said. "Before Buster and I got in the water, I apologized for breaking the rope the other day. He accepted my apology and then we worked out that I would pay more attention to him on the swim. Sometimes I pulled him along, but only if he was OK with it. Sometimes I swam alongside him, making sure he was comfortable with the pace I set."

"And how did that go?" Ashley asked.

"Actually, great," said Christopher. "We finished faster than I expected. Later, when I got in the water with Brit, I was really worried because I'd heard she liked to tread water and talk. So I kind of did the same thing with her. I talked with her ahead of time and we worked some things out. I only pulled her for a little while, and then I went back and talked with her while we made at least some progress through the water."

"You swam and talked at the same time?" Ashley asked.

"Yeah," Christopher said. "Devon had shown her that unusual sidestroke he does. It allows your head to be out of the water most of the time. If you are next to your partner, you can kind of have a conversation while you're swimming."

"Interesting," Ashley said. "And what was it like swimming with Devon?"

"Easy," Christopher said. "He's got to be the easiest tandem partner I've had so far. You'd think that sidestroke would make it hard to swim with him. A scissors kick can really give you a good kick, if it catches you just right. But he almost never kicked me. He seemed to be watching me *and* the shore at the same time. I noticed he adjusts everything he does to how you swim. I think we went just a bit slower than maybe we could have since we were coordinating so carefully, but we made really good progress compared to other teams. And he did a great job with Buster and Brit."

"Really?" Ashley asked. "How did he do that?"

"I don't know, exactly," Christopher said. "I guess he was just adapting to the way they swim. I'm sure he can do other strokes. He did well on day two when we had to do four different strokes around the lily pads. He must just be a good tandem swimmer."

"I wonder where he learned that," Ashley said. "I'd love to ask him where he learned to watch, listen, and coordinate like that."

"Well, we'll probably get a chance to ask him sometime," Christopher said. "I'm sure he'll be asked to stay. He's been in the top half in every swim."

"Yeah, ask him if you see him," Ashley said. "Here comes Robert."

"Hi, Ashley. Hi, Christopher," Robert said as he approached the table.

"Hello," both said back, quietly.

"Ashley, do you have a few moments so I can talk to you?"

"Sure," Ashley said. "Do you mind if Christopher sits in? I'd love to have someone I can share the bad news with."

"Oh. It isn't bad news. But if you want Christopher to hear, I don't mind. As you probably know, your team came in last today, and as you may have also heard, I've asked Jennifer and Andrew to come to my office after lunch."

"Yes, I heard. I'm sorry we did so poorly. I didn't know whether we should get out of the water or not when Andrew walked by, so Emma and I just waited. We were supposed to come out of the water as a team, so I understand if you have to let me go."

"Well, actually, I'm here to ask you to stay. I watched everything that happened in that Challenge. It was clear to me you did everything you could to make your team successful. I saw how you worked with Andrew and were patient enough to get him through his fear of the weeds and out into open water. I saw how you tried your best to keep up with Emma, and even stopped her once while you caught your breath. And I saw how you coaxed Jennifer into swimming the entire time you two were roped together. I know how hard that was because I have it in my notes she didn't do that with anyone else for all four days. When you offered to wait for a teammate, Emma waited with you, even though you could have reasonably guessed you would get a higher score if you got out of the water. She said you talked her into staying. I wanted to talk with you personally so you would understand you didn't just squeak by. We're asking Andrew and Jennifer to leave because we really think it is best for them to find a colony that can fully appreciate what they bring to an organization. But we would really like you to stay until tomorrow. I've watched and you've become one of the most adaptable swimmers out there. You, too, Christopher ... and Devon, though I confess, he had a head start on all of you."

"Wow. Thanks," Ashley said. "I don't know what to say. I guess just 'thanks.' I'm happy to stay. I didn't know if I was doing the right thing or not. I just wanted us to work as a team. But what did you mean by, 'Devon had a head start?'"

"Oh, didn't you know? Devon was raised right here in Good-

PondInc. He's been watching the Challenges his whole life and his parents have prepared him for this since he was a tadpole. We make even our own sons and daughters go through the Challenges. No matter what you are exposed to, there is still no guarantee you can work collaboratively with others until you show it. I can't really talk about another frog's scores, but Devon is not one of the frogs I'm worried about. And neither are you guys, so far."

"Thanks again," Ashley said. "I guess I can only say I hope I get better as I learn from the other frogs."

"Exactly," Robert said. "That is exactly what all of you should be doing. Including you, Christopher. I've got to get going, but enjoy the rest of your lunch. I'll see you by the pond tomorrow morning."

"Of course. Thanks," both Ashley and Christopher said. They were smiling from ear hole-to-ear hole as Robert turned and left the cafeteria.

"Wow," Ashley said. "Can you believe that?"

"Yes, of course," Christopher said. "If there is any colony that would appreciate how you are always willing to work with your teammate, it is GoodPondInc. And I'm happy I can still continue to learn from you."

"Oh, c'mon," Ashley said. "He was saying good things about you too."

"Yes, I guess he was," Christopher said. "At least he was saying I'm not dismissed yet."

"Better *that* than the alternative," Ashley said with a big smile. "Do you want to talk about our lessons today?"

"Sure, let's get them down before we forget 'em," Christopher said. "This was a big day for both of us."

After a few minutes of writing, Ashley looked up to see Christopher patiently waiting.

"I really learned a big lesson today," Christopher said. "It is: 'Everyone has their own style of swimming.' No matter who I partnered with, there was something different about the way they collaborated and worked with me. Fortunately, I think I applied some of the lessons we'd already learned. It even helped, I think, to have swum with Buster before. I knew something about what he was like and I could explain how I wanted to do things differently this morning."

"So, how important do you think it was that you got to talk to him about the swim ahead of time, before you even got in the water?" Ashley asked.

"I guess very important," Christopher answered. "I don't know if he would have gone along with my swimming style if we hadn't discussed it."

"So, I have a line to add to your lesson," Ashley said. "It would read: 'Everyone has their own style of swimming. Share yours. Learn theirs. Manage the swim.'"

"That's great," Christopher said. "Letting other frogs know, right up front, what you plan on doing and how, plus getting them to tell you their style, has got to be a great idea. I never thought of doing that before, but it should be something we do every time. Try to manage the swim by talking about our styles with our partners."

"I ended up doing a little of that when Jennifer and I were talking on top of the lily pad, and later in the water," Ashley said. "We were each learning how to adjust to the other. I think that is a really great lesson."

"So, do you think Eddie would say we'll have to do something like that later, when we're in the colony working on real projects?"

"I would presume so," Ashley said. "I mean, I think 'our style' can mean more than just our swimming style. It could mean how we approach projects, or how we communicate, or how we prioritize and manage our time. Yeah, I think Eddie would want us to remember that."

"Yeah, share your style. Learn theirs. And manage not just the project, but the interactions and collaboration and teamwork between you and your teammates as well." After a brief pause, he added, "So what lessons did you have?"

Ashley said, "I wrote: 'Some frogs won't get in the water. Others will cut the rope. You can only invite frogs into the water – you can't drag them.'"

"Very, very true," Christopher said. "I didn't know Andrew could be so difficult. But I think you did the right thing by not trying to force him. And Jennifer was going to be lazy no matter what any-body did. I guess there are times when you can only make the best of a bad situation. And realize you're only responsible for your own behavior. You can't *make* frogs do what you want them to. You can only invite them."

"Yes, that is exactly what I want to remember," Ashley said. "You can't drag them into the water. If frogs simply don't want to swim with you, they won't."

"Do you think that ever actually happens in GoodPondInc?" asked Christopher. "Do you think even here they have frogs who just don't work well with others?"

"I don't know," said Ashley. "I hope not. But I guess even here sometimes, maybe, frogs get burnt out. Or two frogs are just not a good pair with each other. I'll guess we'll have to ask Eddie that question, next time we see him."

"Yup. That's a great idea. Let's ask Eddie," Christopher said. "Well, I've got to get going. I'm really happy Robert said you weren't going to leave GoodPondInc. You did the best you could today. Hopefully, we'll get to swim together again soon."

"Yeah. I hope so too," Ashley said. "Meanwhile, congratulations on doing so well."

As they got up and walked away, Christopher's mind turned to-ward the training he was about to go to, but Ashley's mind lingered on their conversation. She couldn't stop thinking about Devon. If he had grown up in GoodPondInc and was clearly able to do well on the tandem swim with anybody he was paired with, what was his secret? What did he do specifically, and was it something she and Christopher could learn?

– Chapter Five –

When Christopher arrived at the pond the next morning, he could immediately tell today was going to be different. Out in the middle of the pond were two large nets on top of floating lily pads. The nets were facing each other with a lot of water in between. Robert was gathering up the frogs on the beach and Christopher saw Ashley near the back of the pack.

"Hey, great to see you," Christopher said, waving at the nets. "What do you think this is all about?"

"I don't know, but did you see the ropes? They seem a lot shorter today."

"Oh, I think you're right. This should be interesting," Christopher replied, a little sarcastically.

Just then, Robert blew his whistle to get everyone's attention. "Today, you will be tied to a new partner, as usual. But instead of swimming around the pond, you will be playing a game we call 'grape in the net.' You may have never played this game before, so listen carefully to the rules. The group will be divided into two teams. The goal is for each team to get the grape into the opposing team's net. Each time you do, your team gets a point. The winning team will get to hit the showers first and go to lunch fifteen minutes ahead of the losing team, who will have to stay back and clean up the nets. When you are swimming today, you will have to coordinate carefully with your partner. Both of you will be treading water most of the time. You can raise your arms to try and block a shot or stop a pass by the opposing players, but you can't pull anyone under water. And no dunking. After I assign you your partner and put you on your teams, you will have a few minutes to talk out a strategy with your team. Are there any questions?"

None of the frogs spoke up, so Robert started reading out the pairings. Christopher was paired with a frog called Alyssa. He hadn't heard much about her and wasn't too sure how well she could swim, but she seemed nice when they tied their rope to each other. Ashley was paired with a frog named Chen. She hadn't heard much about him either.

As each team swam past the weeds and out into the deep water, everyone quickly discovered how difficult it was to swim and tread water with someone tied so close. It required extraordinary coordination not to disrupt the other frog's swimming. Ashley and Chen quickly adapted to each other. They had talked a bit on shore and decided to try alternating their arm strokes since they were about the same size. Out in the deep water, it worked pretty well. It was only when the grape was near them and they tried to reach for it simultaneously that their coordination broke down.

As the game began and every tandem started swimming in earnest, Ashley noticed she was getting splashed by Chen. At first she didn't say anything about it, though it was really annoying her, because Chen seemed to make an, "I'm sorry," comment each time he splashed. Conversely, whenever he got splashed himself, he usually said, "That's OK," to Ashley. Very quickly, this made Ashley feel better about being splashed and she started saying the comments back to him. Eventually, both of them realized it was ridiculous to make a comment after every single splash – it was happening way too often. So they stopped making comments and occasionally just smiled at each other, or laughed when the splash caught the other one off guard. By the end, splashing had become a way of teasing each other and neither thought much about it.

Christopher was having a different experience with Alyssa. She was a strong swimmer, so, early in the game, they scored often for their team. However, whenever Christopher splashed Alyssa, she would shoot him a dirty look. At first, he didn't think much of it since he was clearly getting splashed too. *He* wasn't making a big deal out of it, after all. But since they were both trying so hard, they were also clearly disrupting each other's strokes.

About halfway through the game, Alyssa's frustration with Christopher's splashing apparently boiled over and she deliberately splashed Christopher in the face. He was surprised and knew instantly she had done it on purpose. Before he could think about the best way to respond, he reached over and dunked her. She popped back up very fast and just gave him a stare he had never seen before – like she could skin him alive if she only had a knife.

From that point on, she essentially refused to be a participant in the game. Both she and Christopher looked mad. They pulled their rope as tight as it would go and drifted toward the outside edge of the crowd. For minutes, they just treaded water and waited for the end of the game. As they came to shore, neither spoke to each other and they quickly untied their rope before moving to opposite ends of the beach.

On shore, Robert announced that the "green" team, the team Ashley and Chen were on, had won the game, but Christopher and Alyssa's "yellow" team were only one point behind. Half the tandems then headed for the showers and the other tandems gradually gathered up the nets from the middle of the pond. Christopher couldn't believe they had lost by one point. He knew he could have scored more, if Alyssa hadn't taken him out of the game. He shouldn't have dunked her, but she shouldn't have deliberately splashed him. But the big question that bothered him now was: what of the consequences? Did he just drastically hurt his chances of staying at GoodPondInc?

At lunch, Ashley and Christopher joined Eddie and compared their morning experiences. "I don't understand what happened," Christopher said. "How come you and Chen were fine splashing each other and Alyssa basically flipped out?"

"I don't know," Ashley said. "I remember at first I was pretty annoyed, but then Chen started apologizing every time he splashed me. Somehow that helped me understand he didn't mean it on purpose."

"Well, why should I have apologized?" Christopher said. "It was obvious we were going to splash each other some of the time. And she splashed me and didn't apologize. She seemed so nice on shore. How did she get so mean once we got in the water?"

"I really can't help you," Ashley said. "I did think to myself at some point during the swim that if we hadn't talked on shore and gotten to know each other a little bit, it would have been more difficult to accept his splashing. But we got so comfortable with each other that, near the end, we were even splashing each other on purpose, kind of like teasing."

"Well, I can see how splashing can be like teasing. But we clearly never got to that point. After I dunked her, she basically quit."

"You dunked her?" Ashley said, surprised.

"Yeah. It happened so fast. I'm not sure I really intended to. I mean, I did *try* to dunk her, but I didn't plan it or anything. It made her really mad. Essentially we didn't talk or collaborate at all after that."

"I don't know, Christopher," Ashley said. "Maybe I would have done the same thing. If she had been mean to me, I mean. But splashing and teasing is one thing. You can't dunk a frog accidentally. There isn't any way to interpret that except that the other frog wants to be mean to you."

"Yeah. I know you're right," Christopher answered. "I guess I should have apologized, but she made me so mad with her nasty looks. I wasn't in the mood to apologize right then and there. And she splashed me on purpose right before that."

Eddie jumped in at this point and said he wanted to help if he could. Christopher answered, "Gladly". He was still mad from the morning and was worried his team's loss might keep him from being accepted into the colony.

"Don't worry about that, Christopher," answered Eddie. "From what you've told me, you did very well on the other days, and one event won't make the colony kick you out. The supervisors are all trained to look for patterns of behavior and sometimes things just go wrong. However, I want to pick up on something Ashley said earlier. She said splashing was like teasing. Did you really mean that, Ashley?"

"Yes, I think I did," Ashley said. "At least if felt that way. Once we were comfortable with each other, we could tease each other a little bit, and even though someone else might have thought we were being mean, we knew we weren't."

"That's a good lesson to keep in mind as you begin to work in the colony," Eddie said. "Nearly all of our projects involve teamwork, and teasing back and forth is a natural part of our interactions. It can look mean or like sarcasm to an outsider. But in fact, it can help some relationships grow stronger. It takes a certain amount of confidence and trust between two people to feel comfortable teasing. And, of course, sometimes it's just plain fun."

"I know that," Christopher said. "So how come Alyssa didn't see it as natural? Why did she get so mad?"

"Probably because she didn't see it as teasing, or because she wasn't that comfortable with you yet," Eddie said. "Wouldn't you agree it can only be teasing if the other frog interprets it that way? What did it feel like when she intentionally splashed you? Did you take it as teasing?"

"Of course not. She was being rude and intentionally mean."

"See what I mean?" Eddie said.

"Eddie," Ashley interrupted. "Are you saying that sometimes we can do or say the exact same thing, but depending upon how the other person interprets it, we can be perceived as being mean or as being friendly?"

"That's been my experience," Eddie said.

"I certainly thought she was being mean," Christopher said.

"How about we write that down," Ashley said. "I think we've just stumbled upon a very important lesson. I'd like to write: 'Splash and tease only as much as your partner wants.'"

"OK, and I'll add a line," Christopher said. "'And watch for clues you've gone too far.' What I mean by that is, if you don't catch it early, your teasing or splashing is going to get the other frog angry. You might not get the chance to stop and apologize quickly enough."

"Good lesson," Eddie added. "But I think you should go even further. Here in GoodPondInc, we all have to be careful not to let our emotions get the better of us. We don't want to be intentionally mean to someone before we have time think about it."

"Yeah, like that dunk," Ashley said to Christopher.

"OK, so how about I add a new lesson," Christopher said. "This one will read: 'You can accidentally splash, but you can't accidentally dunk.'"

"And add: 'And don't ever dunk!'" Ashley said.

"Christopher, I don't want you to beat yourself up," said Eddie. "You made a simple mistake and we've all done that at one time or another. I know I've done it more than once. What I can offer is that in my experience, it can be fixed. Have you thought about what you are going to say the next time you see Alyssa? You realize you both might end up working in our colony. Eventually, you might have to work with her on a real project."

"Oh, shoot," Christopher said. "No, I hadn't thought of that. I don't know what I'm going to say. I'm still pretty mad. And I'm sure she's still real mad. You should have seen her face."

"It will be all right," Ashley said, trying to sound hopeful.

"Correction, it *can* be all right," Eddie said. "But it doesn't have to be. I've seen tandems come through the Challenges really mad at each other. If one or both of them don't make some effort to get past their anger, they can hold a grudge for a really long time. Sometimes for as long as they work here."

"Oh, no," Christopher said. "I don't really want to be mad at her forever. Like I said, at first I thought she was really nice."

"Have you thought about apologizing to her the next time you see her?" Ashley said.

"Hmm. I have to think about that. It was really her fault we got into such a fight," Christopher said.

"You'll have to think that one out on your own, Christopher," Eddie said. "I don't think Ashley or I can help you with that decision."

"OK, but I don't want to forget this important lesson," Ashley said. "Do you mind if I write down on my pad: 'Someone may have to apologize first?'"

"No, I don't mind," Christopher said. "I guess it just makes sense. If you are going to work with each other again at some point in the future. But I'd add a line – and it will tell you how I *really* feel right now. 'Someone may have to apologize first. Even if they don't *think* they should have to go first.'"

"Good lesson," Eddie commented. "You'll find once you start working here that being a good teammate sometimes means ignoring or quickly getting over small mistakes or 'slights' from a teammate. We all sometimes say the wrong thing, or something we don't really mean. If you can't get over the small stuff, your team will never have a chance to gel. And sometimes, 'getting over it' might mean you do the apologizing, even if you don't think you should."

"But doesn't that mean you've accepted responsibility for the bad thing that happened?" Christopher protested. "What if there is really no way that it was truly your fault?"

"There are ways of saying you are sorry the situation has gotten to this point, without having to say you accept all of the responsibility for how it got that way," said Eddie. "Maybe you can just say, 'I'm sorry we're having so much trouble between us right now, and I'd like to accept my responsibility for the part I played in it.' You could then make reference to miscommunication or a misunderstanding of some kind. Either way, it at least will open the door to repairing the relationship."

"But shouldn't both people accept that responsibility? Shouldn't both be trying to repair the relationship?" asked Christopher.

"Yes, in a perfect world," said Eddie, with an ironic smile playing across his face. "But in this world, sometimes one of the two just has to be the bigger frog."

"Yeah, I guess you're right," Christopher agreed, reluctantly.

"I think you're both getting a lot out of the Challenges," Eddie added. "But I confess, I have to leave lunch a little early today. Is there anything else I can help you with?"

"Not exactly," Ashley said. "But there was one other lesson I knew I wanted to write down today. I found swimming with someone else was hard, with such a short rope between us. It took a lot of concentration and coordination. It was almost as if every stroke and kick I made had to be timed and done in such a way that it would work with Chen."

"I know what you mean," Christopher said. "I really got annoyed when Alyssa didn't think about how her swimming would affect me. She wasn't concentrating real hard on how she moved her arms or legs."

"There seems to be a very good lesson in there somewhere," Eddie said. "How do you want to phrase it?"

"I don't know," Ashley said.

"I do," Christopher said. "It should read: 'When swimming with someone else, every stroke, every splash, every kick … matters. To them.'"

"Great. That sounds like a keeper," Eddie said.

"Yes," agreed Ashley. "We should always keep an eye out for how our behavior is affecting other frogs. We might not think anything of some particular thing we do, but what if they think it's a big deal? We should recognize that and take that into account."

"Yeah," Christopher agreed. "That's what I was getting at. I might think I'm teasing. Or my 'bump' or badly timed joke is no big deal. But maybe they are really getting annoyed with me. I would rather pay attention and try to get a good read on how they are responding to me before I make assumptions."

"That's a really good lesson," Eddie added. "Watching for how other people are responding to you, both verbally and non-verbally, is a really useful skill. If you try, you can get better at it over time. Hey, I've got to run, but keep up the good work. I can't promise anything, of course, but I'm really looking forward to working with both of you when you officially join the colony."

"Thanks," Ashley said.

"Sure thing," Christopher said. But a concerned look came across his face as Eddie left, and he turned to talk to Ashley.

"I know I shouldn't be worried," he said. "It was just two days ago when I came in first place with Emma. But I don't like how poorly Alyssa and I worked together this morning. I'm sure it will lower my evaluation."

"You don't know that," Ashley said. "And besides, in the beginning, you and Alyssa scored more goals than anyone. Perhaps it was just that you both were so competitive you ended up having some kind of tension between the two of you."

"I don't know," Christopher said. "You could be right. But I can't help thinking that somehow Devon would have handled it differently."

"Oh, Devon. I've been meaning to ask you about him. Eddie also mentioned Devon grew up in GoodPondInc. This means he probably knows lots of ways of working with others in a team environment. What do you think he's doing differently that's making him such a good partner?"

"I'm not sure. I know that when I swam with him, he just coordinated with me so well I didn't even feel like I had to do anything special. It was almost natural that there was someone tied to my waist. By far he's been the easiest partner I've had."

"I'm really curious how he did that," Ashley said. "Don't you think if we knew what he was doing, we could really get better at working with others?"

"Sure. But I haven't seen him at lunch today and he seems kind of quiet when we get to the beach each morning."

"Yes, I don't know when we're going to get a chance to talk to him, but let's make a pact. If either one of us gets a chance to corner him, we'll share with the other what we learned."

"OK. Sounds like a plan. By the way, do you think we're adapting enough that we'll both get into GoodPondInc? Sometimes I feel really confident, but other times I think I just don't have this cooperating thing down."

"I'm sure. I think both of us have one quality that makes us a bit different from the others. We're eager to learn and adapt. We're learning to manage ourselves. That's got to be a good thing, right?"

"Yeah. That sounds right. But I don't find working with others as easy as you do. I'd rather focus on getting the Challenge done fast and right. And sometimes I think it's all right to stretch the rope."

"Well, maybe that's one of your strengths. We can't all just be loafing around treading water, can we?"

"Nope. Speaking of that, I just noticed the time. I've got to run."

"Me too. Keep your eye out for Devon. There's got to be something he can teach us."

"Will do. See you tomorrow, if not before." But as Christopher headed for the door, a new question popped into his head – one he was careful not to let show on his face. If Ashley was so focused on coordinating with others and keeping the rope slack, was she succeeding only because her partners were focused on completing the task? Were they essentially carrying her workload? How could a relationship-oriented frog like Ashley ever fit in at such a productive workplace as GoodPondInc?

– Chapter Six –

As Ashley approached the pond the next morning, there was a thick fog over everything. She had a hard time finding Christopher and almost stumbled into him. He was at the side of the beach talking to Devon. She could tell he must have asked Devon what he felt were the most important lessons he had learned growing up in GoodPondInc.

"I can't say it's just one thing," Devon said. "Certainly I watched my Mom and Dad a lot as they went about raising me and my fellow tadpoles. They were good communicators, I recall. Always talking out their differences. Dad was more focused on getting things done and Mom was always worrying about her relationships – we call that 'her ropes' in GoodPondInc."

"Her ropes?" asked Christopher.

"Yeah. I think it's a holdover from the Challenges. Since everyone at GoodPondInc has been through the Challenges, they use that shared experience as a way to talk about how to work together. Mom was a relationship person. She didn't like broken or frayed ropes."

"Well, that kind of reminds me of my friend Ashley here. Have you two met yet? Ashley, this is Devon."

"No, we haven't," Ashley said. "I heard you swam with Christopher the other day?"

"Yes, we did the swim where you had to switch off with three different partners," Devon said.

"You did very well," Ashley said. "I don't want to interrupt you guys. You were saying you learned tandem swimming from your Mom and Dad?"

"Well, kind of," Devon said. "We didn't really practice swimming tied to each other. But my Mom and Dad always taught me to be an adaptable partner. Swim a different way if I had to to match the frog I was swimming with. Eventually, I just learned to swim sidestroke so I could watch the other swimmer."

"So that's what you were doing," Christopher said. "It makes sense now. You somehow managed to make it easy to swim with you. I can't recall even one time we bumped legs or our arms crossed."

"Thanks. It was easy swimming with you, too," Devon said. "But I don't always do the sidestroke. Sometimes, when the other person is really swimming hard, I have to put my head in the water just like everyone else and swim as fast as I can."

"But how did you do so well with Brit?" Ashley asked. "She's known as quite a talker. I can't imagine you had any trouble keeping up with her."

"No," Devon said with a slight chuckle. "She wasn't swimming that fast. With teammates like her, it sometimes feels like I'm only treading water. But we still made some progress. Sometimes I gradually pulled her and sometimes we just stopped and treaded water for a while. But really, you can't drag a frog through the water, so what else are you going to do?"

"I guess that makes sense," Ashley said. "I never thought about all of the different kinds of swimmers there are. Nor how much I might have to adapt to them."

"Yeah, but what about those rope-focused frogs," Christopher said, hoping he would learn something that could help him with Ashley, or maybe she would hear it herself.

"Umm. What do you mean?" Devon asked.

"How do you help the relationship-oriented frogs get to the goal quicker? Don't they slow you down? Don't you try to speed them up?"

"Well, not exactly," Devon said. "Getting the Challenge completed isn't the only important thing. Getting it done together, arriving together, is also the most important thing."

"How can you have two most important things?" Christopher asked.

"I don't know. It's just the way it is at GoodPondInc," Devon said. "Get it done, and get it done together. The bottom line is you have to be concerned with both, equally. Though my Dad was more of a task-oriented frog, he didn't ignore relationships. He took his time whenever he needed to. And frogs really enjoyed working with him. Keeping the relationship goal front and center was just something he had to work on a little more. It came more naturally to my Mom."

"So how was your Mom at getting things done?" Christopher asked.

"Just fine, I think," Devon said. "I never heard anyone say she was lazy, if that's what you mean. She would spend a little bit more time talking or worrying about the rope than my Dad, but she worked on staying organized and focused on the task just as hard as my Dad worked on keeping his relationships healthy."

"So, you're saying, whichever one you are stronger at, you might have to work more deliberately on the other?"

"Yeah. I guess that's it," Devon said.

"What I hear you saying," Ashley said, "is it's about working efficiently and getting there as fast as you can, but only when neither of you is really damaging the rope."

"OK, that sounds right too," Devon said. "But remember to relax. And have fun when you can. There's no reason not to enjoy the frogs you're swimming with. When you get into GoodPondInc, you will spend a lot of time with them."

Just then, they were interrupted by Robert's shouting. "Frogs, let's gather around. I don't know how many of you know, but this is the last Challenge for you trainees." An excited murmur spread through the crowd and each frog looked around to see what frogs were left. "As usual, you will be partnered with another frog, but the Challenge will be to swim across the entire pond. I know you can't see the other side today, but each of you will be given a colored rope. When you get to the other side, you will have to find a colored grape that matches your rope. Swim back and bring it here to me. The frogs that get here first will get the best scores. The one difference today is we are going to use the shorter ropes we used during the grape game yesterday. You are going to be very close to each other, so you will have to show excellent collaboration with your partner. Does anyone have any questions before I read out the pairings?"

"Yes," said a frog near the front. "We can't even see the other side. How are we supposed to know where to swim?"

"I can't help that it's foggy today," Robert said. "It's usually foggy this time of year. We still do the Challenges. You aren't the first group to have to swim in the fog. I suggest you talk with your partner before you begin. And remember, getting it done is important, but getting it done together is also important."

As if on cue, Ashley and Christopher both looked over at Devon. It seemed Robert had said almost exactly what Devon had said moments earlier. Both Ashley and Christopher made a mental note to write down this lesson when they saw each other at lunch.

For the last Challenge, Christopher was paired with a frog named Sofia and Ashley was paired with a frog named Diego. As they tied their ropes to each other, Sofia made the first comment to Christopher.

"I don't know about this," she said. "I'm not really fond of fog."

"I know," Christopher said. "But it can't be that bad. We've swum in this pond for the last five days. There can't be anything dangerous out there or they wouldn't let us swim all the way across."

"Maybe," Sofia said. "But we can't even see the other side. How are we supposed to know where to aim?"

"I guess we just go somewhere in that general direction," Diego interjected, waiving his arm toward the other shoreline. "What's the difference if we can see the shore or not? We still have to swim toward the middle. So let's just get started."

"Umm. I kind of agree with Sofia," Ashley said. "It seems a little bit scarier than before. I don't know about swimming with a frog I just met toward a goal I can't even see yet. I'm not sure where we're going or how we're even going to get there."

"Yeah, I see your point," Christopher said. "But what are we going to do instead? Just stand here?" Just then Robert blew his whistle.

"Come on, guys," Diego said. "It's not that bad. If you ask me, the worst part is just getting through the weeds."

Uh oh, thought Ashley. Not another Andrew. A guy afraid of the weeds. But she said out loud to Christopher, "I'm not being indecisive. I'm just being cautious."

"Well, what do you propose we do?" Christopher asked, getting more anxious as frogs kept entering the water ahead of them.

"Well, does one of us have better eyesight? Can anyone see the lily pad field we know is in the middle of the pond?" Ashley said.

"Yeah, just barely," Sofia said. "So what?"

"I can't even see that," Ashley said.

"Me neither," Christopher said.

"Or me," Diego said.

"So, why don't you lead all of us, Sofia," Ashley said. "At least you can get us to the middle of the pond. Then we can talk about what to do after that."

"Me lead?" Sofia exclaimed. "I'm the one most scared because of the fog!"

"We'll be right beside you," Ashley said, reassuring her. "Diego and I will swim as close to you as we can so you won't be alone. We'll make sure we won't get separated. We'll be there if anything should happen."

"That makes sense to me," Christopher said. "I don't mind if you lead, Sofia. I'll swim sidestroke like my friend Devon taught me, and we'll let you do whatever stroke you want so you can keep your head up."

"Well," Sofia said. "I'm not sure this is going to work. But you guys are obviously braver than I am. If you're going to be right there beside me – and no splashing, Christopher ... I guess I'll give it a try."

"Great," Ashley said. "Let's go. We don't want to be the last ones in the water on this Challenge."

As they walked to the water, Diego brought up the topic of weeds again. "Guys, I'm really uncomfortable about starting. I've always found the weeds the most difficult part of these tandem swims. And I've never swum with Ashley before. I don't even know how we're going to coordinate our movements and breathing."

"I agree, the first part has always been the hardest part for me, too," Christopher said. "I seem to bump my partner most while we're still figuring out how to get through the weeds. It's never been fun."

"OK," Ashley said, "but we can't get to open water until we get through the weeds. So let's just be extra careful about how we're affecting our partners' swimming. Take a 'time out' if anyone needs to. We certainly don't want our rope to get caught on a strong weed and break before we get to open water."

"That makes sense," Diego said, "but you might have to be extra careful with me – while we're in the weeds. I have a history of freaking out a little whenever a weed touches me. I don't mean to damage our rope, but it has happened in the past."

"That's actually good to know," Ashley said. "I'll be extra careful. Just let me know how you're doing whenever you can. I'm sure we'll get through the beginning of the swim OK. I'll do everything I can to keep our rope intact."

The four frogs gradually made their way out into the foggy water. Christopher and Ashley paid special attention to their partners' swimming styles and did everything they could to make it easy on their partners. Christopher was able to keep up with Sofia using the sidestroke. He swam slowly and made sure his arms and legs almost never interfered with Sofia's strokes.

Ashley was between Diego and the other tandem, so she had to swivel her head around trying to adjust to Diego *and* keep them close to Christopher and Sofia. She noticed Diego seemed unable or unwilling to try and match her stroke. Several times, she had to pull him back toward the other tandem. On other occasions, he ended up pulling her in his direction. At least twice, when her air was running out, she tugged on the rope and had him stop while she took a breath. Meanwhile, Christopher was gently pulling Sofia along and the group picked up speed. Pretty soon, they could see the lily pads growing in the middle of the pond.

At the lily pads, Christopher suppressed his urge to tell everyone to hurry along. He could see there were several tandems ahead of them, but he could also see some were behind. He thanked Sofia for allowing him to pull on her rope and suggested she should now feel comfortable doing her fastest stroke. They could all now see the far shore. She agreed and, after catching her breath, they slipped off the lily pad and started to swim faster. Their grape was on the far left side of the beach, so Christopher and Sofia headed off in that direction.

Meanwhile, Ashley explained to Diego it would really make it easier for her if he would occasionally lift his head and check on how she was doing. Not that she was doing badly, she explained, but sometimes he was pulling her so hard her face was going under water. She added that also, sometimes, his kicks were knocking her arm. He said he was glad she said something about it. He didn't want to make the swim hard on her. He promised to be more careful, particularly about those two things, and they set off toward their grape on the right side of the beach.

The two teams swam separately through the rest of the Challenge. When they returned to the first shore, they were surprised to find they had finished numbers two and three, respectively.

"I should have known you would finish first," Christopher said to Devon. He and his partner were untying their rope as Christopher and Sofia walked out of the water.

"Hey, you did great," Devon said. "And you barely finished ahead of your friend Ashley. She's right behind you."

"Yeah, we made great time once we got the hang of it," Ashley said. "But that was a really long tandem swim."

"The longest," Devon said. "They say the last day is always the hardest Challenge. I thought the shorter rope and the longer swim made this the hardest swim yet."

"And carrying a grape while tandem swimming," Christopher said.

The three of them walked toward the showers after turning in their ropes and grapes to Robert. "I don't know about you guys," Christopher said, "but I feel pretty comfortable right now that at least the three of us made it in to the colony."

"I don't know," Ashley said. "I can't seem to get any read on Robert. I don't really know how they scored us, other than our finishing order in each Challenge."

"She's at least a little bit right," Devon said. "GoodPondInc cares about the quality and speed of your work, but also how you work with others, your attention to relationships. How well you succeed here is very dependent upon how you are as a teammate. They watch those things. But I wouldn't worry. I think you both did better and better as the week went on."

"Yeah," Christopher said. "I certainly don't know how all of the other teams behaved in the water. Maybe they were just naturally better than us. But Ashley and I really worked at it. We tried to learn how to adapt to our partners. Don't you think so, Ashley?"

"Oh, yes, big time," Ashley said. "Really, even if we don't make it into the colony, I think I'm going to remember some of these lessons for the rest of my life. That reminds me. We can still meet at lunch, can't we, and share what we learned today?"

"Sure," Christopher said. "I wouldn't want to miss that. You always seem to learn something different than I do. I want to compare notes."

As they went their separate ways, Christopher was feeling confident. And proud that he had accommodated Sofia so well during their tandem swim. But he still worried about Ashley. Even though her tandem had come in right behind him, he wondered if she had finally learned to speak up for herself. Or was she just brave and outspoken on the shore, when the rope wasn't really at risk of breaking? Was it possible for her to break out of her passive style?

But Christopher was a bit more worried about one other thing: did he change his aggressive style enough to earn a place in Good-PondInc? And, what did Robert think?

At lunch, Eddie waved Christopher over. He could see Ashley was already at that table. Eddie said he was sorry they had to swim through the fog this morning, but he was eager to hear what Christopher had thought of the swim.

"I couldn't wait," Ashley said. "I already shared with him one of my important lessons from the morning. I wrote on my pad: 'Sometimes just getting through the early weeds is the most difficult part.'"

"Oh, I get it," Christopher said. "Diego sure had a thing about weeds. But at least he wasn't as bad as your other partner, Andrew. What were you saying to him that got him to go willingly?"

"I just said that I would go at whatever pace he wanted. I would be patient if he accidentally kicked or splashed me. I told him I was committed to getting through the weeds with him together. I wasn't going to leave him behind or let the rope break."

"Wow. You told him all that, even before you got in the water?" Christopher said.

"I think that's great," Eddie said. "Many times, here in the colony, the early part of teamwork is the hardest part. Some frogs have been burned in the past by their previous partners, so they are 'weeds shy,' as we say. They don't even want to try because something may have stung them or broken their rope before. On those occasions, what you did, Ashley, is exactly what I would hope any of us at GoodPondInc would do."

"Thanks, Eddie. I confess I wouldn't have done it on the first day. But talking over these teamwork lessons has certainly given me more courage to talk things out if I sense there's a problem."

"Yes, but how did the two of you do in the water?" Christopher asked.

"Very well," Ashley said. "At first, Diego wasn't paying much attention to me, so I tried to be assertive, like Eddie said. I stopped him and told him what I needed. He listened, and he started to do some things differently. Pretty soon, we were making real progress through the water."

"Congratulations, Ashley," Eddie said. "And of course, you accommodated him, I imagine. It's what you naturally do. But, you asked him to accommodate you. That was the part I knew took some special courage from you."

"Yes. And it worked," answered Ashley. "I mean, Christopher was obviously the strongest swimmer of all of us. And he could pull Sofia, so they could go pretty fast. But we finished only a little bit behind him. By the way, how did that go for you, Christopher?"

"Pretty well," Christopher said. "I remembered what Devon said about how task and goal-oriented frogs like me have to put extra work into being more relationship-oriented. Whenever I got impatient with Sofia, or afraid we were losing ground to other teams, I asked myself, 'What would Ashley do?' I simply tried to do that with Sofia. I wanted to keep the rope healthy. *And* get the Challenge done."

"Wow, I'm impressed," Eddie said. "And do you feel like you did that as well as you could?"

"Umm. Well ... not as well as I could with more practice," Christopher said. "But it felt good. I remember when Buster and I finished the Challenge on the first day. We didn't even want to look at each other. But Sofia was fine with me when we finished. She even started to splash me as we came out of the water. I think she and I were beginning to have fun."

"So what lesson are you going to write down today?" Ashley asked.

"I thought of Sofia as I was writing this down: 'Sometimes you both know exactly where you are headed. Sometimes you can't even see the other shore. Try to get good at both situations.' And then I added: 'But the second demands more courage.'"

"That's a great lesson," Ashley said. "She seemed very concerned about the fog and not knowing where she was headed. More worried than most. But you adapted and handled it well."

"Actually, you adapted," Christopher said. "It was you who recognized what she needed was courage. And you suggested an intermediate goal, one she could see. It reduced her anxiety enough she could get in the water." He turned to Eddie. "It was brilliant how Ashley suggested we look at our different abilities and see whether one of us should lead at that time. Turns out one of us did have something – better eyesight."

"That was a great idea," Eddie said. "Did Sofia seem more ready to swim after you talked all this out?"

"She seemed so," Ashley said. "I remembered Devon talking about how different some swimmers are. Some are more afraid. Some are stronger swimmers. And I remembered one of our earlier lessons about managing the swim. I figured if we talked some things out ahead of time, maybe we would all have a better swim. Which I think we did."

"We *certainly* did," Christopher said. "That 'talking it out ahead of time' thing was brilliant. Is brilliant!"

"Eddie," asked Ashley, "can you think of any important lesson we're missing? I know we don't have to do any more Challenges, but like you said, there are a lot of similarities between the Challenges and the kinds of things we might have to do in GoodPondInc. Presuming, of course, we get asked to stay."

"Umm. There is one thing I wanted to make sure both of you understood, now that you've done all of these different Challenges, with all of these different partners. I would add one more lesson to your pad: 'Every challenge is different, yet the goal is always the same: arrive together.'"

"Yeah, I agree. That's a great lesson," Christopher said.

"Me too," Ashley said. They both added it to their lists and counted down the minutes until lunch was over. So far, neither one had been called to Robert's office.

At five o'clock, Ashley and Christopher both received invitations to come to the grassy area in front of the main building. When they arrived, they discovered the entire colony had gathered around the edges of the field and Robert was standing in the middle. He called each of the trainee frogs to the middle and made a brief presentation, congratulating them on making it through the colony's trainee program. There were nearly a dozen frogs lined up on the grass as the entire colony came by and shook each hand, accepting them into the colony. Both Ashley and Christopher were smiling from ear hole-to-ear hole as Eddie came through the line.

"Congratulations to both of you. I really had no worries both of you would make it," Eddie said.

"Well, I was certainly worried," Christopher said.

"Me too," Ashley said. "But I really want to thank you for your help. Those lessons you had us write down were very helpful. I thought of them a lot."

"Me too," Christopher said. "I learned a lot through this program. I'm sure I'm going to learn even more as I work in the colony."

"Probably," Eddie said. "What do you think was the most important lesson you took away from the Challenges?"

"That's hard to say," Ashley said. "I probably have two dozen lessons written on my pads. What do you think, Christopher?"

"Umm. I'm not sure either," Christopher said.

"I can help with that," Robert said. He had come up from behind Ashley and Christopher and had heard Eddie's question. "By the way, it seems like you've already met Eddie. I'm really happy about that. In a way, Eddie is the most valuable member of our colony."

"Really?" Ashley asked.

"Sure," Robert said. Eddie started to protest, but Robert cut him off. "What all of us know is that Eddie is the best in the colony at working with any one of us. He can adapt to everyone's style. He's productive yet always concerned about keeping the relationship healthy. If there is any one thing you should take away from the Challenges, it is that the most successful swimmers can swim with anyone – whether leading, following, or just treading water."

"Well, I wouldn't call me the most valuable member of the colony," Eddie said. "There are many of us who can do that, but I agree with Robert's conclusion. GoodPondInc's success is definitely due to our ability, and our desire, to keep both goals in mind; get the task done and keep the relationship healthy. And that means adapting to each other, best we can."

"I get it," Christopher said.

"Me too," Ashley said. "I am definitely going to add that to my pad: 'The most successful swimmers can swim with anyone. Whether leading, following, or just treading water.' Imagine if we hadn't gone through the Challenges?" she asked Christopher. "We wouldn't have learned that!"

"Yeah, but I have to say, I'm glad it's over," Christopher said. "That wasn't easy, having to swim with someone else tied to you every day."

"Over?" Eddie said. "Didn't anyone tell you?"

"Oh. I may have forgotten to mention it," Robert said, with a wry smile. "That was only your initial training. There is still more training to do, now that you are full members of the colony."

"Oh," Ashley said. "We have to do more tandem swims?"

"In the mornings?" Christopher asked.

"Not right away," Robert said.

"No, but down the road," Eddie said. "So keep those lessons handy. You may want to add to them before your next tandem swims."

Both Ashley and Christopher looked at each other and gave weak smiles. Working in this colony was going to be tough. But they could tell by the looks on each other's faces, they wouldn't want it any other way.

84   Erick J. Lauber

– Appendix –

Someone asked me after reading an early draft of this book, "Why a parable? Wouldn't it have been shorter and more direct to just tell people what you wanted them to learn?"

"Yes," I had to answer. "It would have. But I don't think it would have worked as well." I went on to explain that I've been teaching both communications and leadership for years. Through classes, training seminars, and workshops, I've been trying to help people remember the basic principles of successful collaboration, effective communication, and cooperative teamwork in a hundred different ways. But I've worried that all of those complicated acronyms and fancy phrases have gone unremembered in the moments when they would have been most useful: in a heated discussion at work or the anxious moments of deciding how to react to a colleague. I even find it hard to remember my own teachings when I'm going about my normal, busy day.

Then it dawned on me: use a metaphor. Find some easily re-membered picture or activity that can guide people when they are about to enter a difficult situation at work or are dreading an emotional, high-stakes conversation. Hence, the metaphor of being tied at the waist to someone and having to swim across a channel or large pond. Accomplishing the task is clearly important, but you must do it while coordinating and swimming alongside someone else. And both of you must arrive together!

Then I thought long and hard about how I could expand this metaphor to help with the various difficulties one might experience at work. After much effort, I found a way to map dozens of my lessons into this simple and easily remembered metaphor. Then …

I thought of frogs. The rest came easily. My basic lesson is: when faced with a difficult situation or difficult colleague at work, just imagine you have to swim across a pond with this person tied to your waist. You will have to coordinate with them and be considerate of them, and they will have to do the same to you, but importantly, you have to arrive together – you can't break the rope! But the metaphor can mean even more than that.

First, obviously, the rope is your relationship with that other person. It can be long or short. You may have to work closely with that person, or hardly at all. It can be healthy, frayed, or broken. Because it's made of lily pad stem, it can be repaired, but only if you are in the water, swimming together. It doesn't repair itself on land, when you stay away from the other person. So the first lesson that Ashley and Christopher learn is, "Don't break the rope!" The organization does not want its employees/teammates unable to work together. Ever! Breaking your relationship with a teammate is never an acceptable behavior to the organization as a whole.

Second, there are different kinds of people in the world. Some will want to lead. Some are more passive. Sometimes both want to be in charge. The interactions between people affect the rope. It can be frustrating if you don't understand how or why someone else is acting the way they are. Particularly if you think their behavior is harming either the task or the rope. If one of the two people is not paying any attention to how the other is feeling, then this will become a major issue, i.e. the disrespected person may feel like they are being dragged underwater and cannot get enough air. Respect is like air – if you feel like you don't have enough of it, it becomes all you can think about.

For people like Christopher, who are naturally more task-oriented, learning to watch how teammates are reacting and behaving is very important. Task-focused people may need to slow down or give up a turn at leadership so that others can feel valued and respected. Importantly, as Eddie stated, "Nearly everything we do is group work, one way or another." Keeping the relationship intact is the responsibility of everyone, including the task-oriented types.

I feel these are the two most important lessons of the book, and they are front and center in Chapter One.

In Chapter Two, Christopher and Ashley discover they have different personalities. Christopher is more aggressive and Ashley is more passive. This creates frustrations for both. Christopher is not paying enough attention to Ashley's non-verbal communication, so she feels slighted, under-valued, disrespected. Ashley is not contributing enough to the swim by volunteering to step up and take the lead so Christopher thinks she is not trying hard enough. He's also annoyed she doesn't bring up her concerns, though it's probably because she doesn't want to make him mad. Ultimately, Christopher feels the task takes priority over anyone's temporary feelings. So why didn't she raise her issues in the heat of the moment, when it might have done some good? Importantly, neither understands why the other doesn't think and act like they do.

In my experience, many, many people in the workplace can be located on one end or the other of this continuum. What it demands from each is the ability to be flexible and a willingness to accept that others can be different without being "evil" or "bad." We get mad at people when we interpret their behavior as arising from "ill intent." I believe we need to let go of that interpretation, or at least reserve it for very, very rare occasions. In truth, nearly all of us need to move toward "assertiveness" – communicating our thoughts, needs, beliefs, and desires effectively to others while respecting that others have an equal right to communicate their thoughts, needs, beliefs, and desires effectively to us. The "Ashleys" of the world need to speak up more, and the "Christophers" need to listen and value more the thoughts, needs, beliefs, and desires of others.

These principles can be easy to remember in the context of the tandem swimming metaphor. For example, Ashley needs to remember to speak up and lead more: "It takes courage to swim hard and tug on the rope, if you are not used to leading." And, as Christopher added, "Pulling on the rope sometimes means you are helping the team." Don't always be so afraid of hurting the relationship that you don't ever say a potentially negative thing, or voice a disagreement with your partner – particularly if that communication will help accomplish the task. Try to remember – the rope can withstand a few tugs, and if you have an assertive or aggressive teammate, they will understand the need to pull on the rope sometimes.

For Christopher, the lesson was, "Watch and listen – make sure everyone is getting enough air." In real life, this really means "getting enough respect" – being valued. The second part of that lesson was, "And if the other is not getting enough air, stop and do something about it." To the "Christophers" I have to say, "Don't be so task-oriented that you don't occasionally give the rope – the relationship – top priority."

For Ashley, the lesson was that despite her frustrations and feelings of "lack of respect," it was not appropriate for her to just quit. Relationship-oriented people sometimes allow their feelings toward co-workers to sabotage their work. They shut down or direct their energies elsewhere. This isn't healthy for the organization as a whole. No one should ever just quit and make others "drag" them. And perhaps, equally bad, some people who cannot find their voice while working with someone, find their voice later – when the partner is not around. "Holding your breath until later" is not the best approach either. Sometimes assertiveness is exactly what is needed by the more relationship-oriented teammate. They need to learn to speak up more.

Christopher's last lesson in that chapter is to ask himself, "Could it be my fault if I'm always doing all of the pulling?" Aggressive types may need to consciously change their behavior if they are frustrated by their teammates' behaviors. Perhaps they can coax their partners into more leadership-/task-behaviors. Aggressives may have to ask themselves, "What can I do to get better performance from the team as a whole, not just how can I perform better?" Of course, as Ashley rightly points out, it is a two-way street. But Christopher can ultimately only control his own behavior. If he pulls too much on someone's rope, they may eventually quit. He'll have to learn how to adapt his style.

In Chapter Three, I explored some general phenomena that can happen during teamwork. For example, occasionally you get splashed. Sometimes what the other person does or says does not sit well with you. It could be just the way they swim (communicate). Some people are just not as adept at working with others as the "socially skilled." Sometimes it may be due to tiredness, or anxiety, or any number of physical or psychological reasons – all of which translate to that other person did not intend to splash you. Remember, splashes and even kicks are going to occur when people tandem swim. Try not to draw the worst possible interpretation each time. Meanwhile, no one likes getting splashed or kicked in the face, so try to swim side-by-side. Try to be as equal as possible and watch how you communicate. It makes it easier on everybody.

On the other hand, sometimes people do need to stop and "tread water," either because they just don't have the stamina or because they feel the relationship (the rope) could use a little "healing" at that point. Task-oriented types will need to relax and allow that to occur. But, of course, the relationship-oriented will need to recognize that "treading water" is not the same as making progress toward the goal. Some people will sit and chat all day long if you let them. Thus, some middle ground is necessary between socializing too long, and not socializing enough.

Later in Chapter Three, Ashley and Christopher learn that, "Tandem swims require a lot of patience." This may not be a surprise, but the second part of that lesson is the hardest for task-oriented people to remember: "But at least you arrive together." The organization always wants the rope to stay healthy between teammates, or at least intact. Arriving together is just as important as arriving at all. This may mean people have to take turns leading. But it also means that relationship-oriented people need to help out as much as they can, even when they are not leading. It is usually true that long, complicated projects will require every person to lead at some point. Conversely, aggressive types need to remember they can't always be in charge. "Patience" should be at the forefront of their consciousness.

In Chapter Four, both learn that there are all kinds of people in the world. Christopher makes this his first lesson: "Everyone has their own style of swimming," i.e. everyone has their own style of communicating and collaborating. But Ashley adds an important addendum to his lesson: "Share yours. Learn theirs. Manage the swim." The take-home message is that the more we can explain how we swim to our prospective teammates, and the more we learn about how they swim, the better we can manage everyone's expectations and start to coordinate more quickly. This may allow us to head off future issues, perhaps solving them while no one is angry – yet. By sharing and learning everyone's work habits, communication styles, issues that have been problems in the past … we can manage the collaboration better.

Jennifer, for example, just won't do any work. Even though she is capable, she is unmotivated. This causes Ashley to drag her. However, this creates an opportunity for Ashley to lead and, partly because she is forced to, she realizes she can lead. Also, given her natural tendency to avoid confrontation, she doesn't make a big deal out of Jennifer's behavior. However, Christopher is just plain mad when he has to drag someone. He can't stand to have a partner who doesn't try, particularly if it affects his success. Fortunately, by the time he gets to lunch, he's resigned himself to the lesson that, "You can't make other people swim." You can't force an outstanding effort from a teammate. Sometimes you can only make the best of a bad situation. But Robert, who represents the voice of the organization, explains that the larger team appreciates your continued effort. He recognizes that not everyone is the best collaborator, but making your best effort is what the organization hopes and expects.

In Chapter Four, Ashley and Christopher also meet Devon, an excellent collaborator. He has mastered how to get things done and keep relationships healthy. This allows them to recognize that many times when people join a team, there already exist role models and potential mentors within the organization. Ashley and Christopher consciously decide to watch and learn from Devon. What can they emulate? What does he do differently? One of the first things they discover is that he "swims" with his head up, watching how his teammate is swimming, even while he is making progress toward the goal. This lesson will get reinforced in the later chapters.

In Chapter Five, Ashley and Christopher learn what it's like to work so closely with someone that even their little behaviors, their tiny splashes, become annoying. In Christopher's case, his dedication to winning means he doesn't pay much attention to how his behavior is affecting Alyssa. At least not until she deliberately splashes him back. Of course, not realizing what part he may have had in annoying her, he reacts badly: he dunks her. This pretty much ruins the relationship. Alyssa effectively shuts down.

When we strike out at people at work, even when we think we've been provoked, we can essentially shut down the relationship, even if the other person doesn't formally break the rope. Turning to verbal violence or outright attacks on another person never helps the team. It is never what the larger organization wants. So the question becomes, are you going to do what your anger wants you to do, or are you going to do what's best for the team?

On the other hand, if relationships are allowed to grow naturally, if two people discover gradually that their teasing and joking are accepted by the other person, then what might look like "splashing" to a third party might be just fine between the two people. Sometimes, in fact, depending upon their personalities, it might even be fun and a large part of why they enjoy coming to work. But it's very person-specific. New teammates will have to make it very, very clear early in their relationship that they mean no harm and they are only trying to have some fun. And they'll have to be willing to get splashed back. In general, as Ashley and Christopher learn, "Splash and tease only as much as your partner wants, and look for clues you've gone too far."

Chapter Five is where Christopher learns that some behaviors are still off limits. There are still inappropriate behaviors in the workplace, even if you might think they are funny or OK. Learn and follow the boundaries of social behavior in your organization. Crossing the line and "dunking" will always get a bad reaction.

Of course, sometimes relationships deteriorate – accidentally, or perhaps someone cuts the rope. Unfortunately, in the real world, there are some very tough choices to make, like, "Do I apologize first or do I (in my opinion) justifiably wait for them?" It is in essence the difference between letting the rope stay broken, or doing something to give it at least a chance to heal. As Christopher discovers, sometimes you have to go first, even if you don't think you should have to. Importantly, he hears from the senior members of the team that giving the rope a chance to heal is always what the organization wants. Every organization wants teammates who can work together, pull in the same direction. True, the "Ashleys" of the world may end up apologizing more than they should. But the "Christophers" are the ones who really need to hear that sometimes they just have to apologize first. In a perfect world, Eddie says, perhaps both people would work hard toward repairing the relationship. "But in this world, sometimes one of the two just has to be the bigger frog."

At the end of Chapter Five, Ashley and Christopher come to the realization that, "When swimming together" – when working closely with someone – "every stroke, every splash, every kick … matters. To them." We need to concentrate on our words and behaviors because everything we do around another person is an act of communication – and how it is received influences what they do next, and how healthy the rope is.

In Chapter Six, the excellent collaborator, Devon, explains how his father and mother encouraged him at a very young age to work things out with people, and to pay attention to how his "strokes and kicks" were affecting other people's performances. Unfortunately, not all of us have had such excellent role models. We may have picked up bad habits from the past. Patterns of behavior that were unconsciously learned but still get triggered by something in our environment. Have you ever heard yourself sound like your mom or your dad, particularly when you're angry or annoyed? Devon's lesson is that we can all learn how to swim sidestroke, if we deliberately try.

Meanwhile, in this chapter, Ashley is confronted with another person "afraid of the weeds" – someone who doesn't want to even get in the water and start a collaboration. Some of these people will be fine once they get past the initial awkwardness of starting the work and getting to know their partner. But perhaps bad experiences in the past have made them "weed shy." This means for Ashley that she will have to start out slow – be patient. In Chapter Six, her natural concern for relationships allows her to handle this situation well. Note, it would have been a much more difficult dilemma for Christopher. Going forward, he is going to have to remember that for some people, "Just getting through the weeds is the most difficult part."

The "swim" in Chapter Six is to accomplish a task with an unclear or undefined goal. This can be a special challenge to collaborations. It usually takes more talking it out up front, and perhaps brainstorming and decision making before the real work even begins. We all know that for some, this is not a real problem – they will just jump right in and get started. But for others, their anxiety might be higher than normal because they are not clear about what to do or they lack confidence in their competence. Christopher recognizes that an excellent collaborator would have to become good at both situations. They would have to be flexible about jumping right in or taking the time to learn what everyone brings to the task and their style. For some, not "seeing the other shore" demands extra courage. "Thinking like an Ashley," being more relationship-oriented, is sometimes required of natural-born "Christophers."

Near the end of the chapter, Eddie reinforces one of the most important lessons of the book: "Every challenge is different, yet the goal is always the same – arrive together." The overall health and success of the organization is increased when everyone can work together, get the task done, and keep a healthy rope between them. Perhaps not surprisingly, Robert reveals at the end that Eddie is himself an excellent role model for Ashley and Christopher. He can adapt to anyone in the organization, whether they are leading, following … or just treading water!

About the Author

Dr. Erick J. Lauber received his Ph.D. in Psychology from the Univ. of Michigan Psychology Department over 20 years ago and has been teaching, training and producing educational materials ever since. His scholarship has appeared in over 100 journals, magazines and book chapters, and his media products have won over two dozen national awards.

In 2004 he joined the faculty of Indiana Univ. of Pennsylvania and has since taught communications, journalism and leadership, both on- and off-campus, to thousands. He has been a leader/president of numerous for-profit companies and non-profit organizations, and has won both regional and national leadership awards. Most recently, he has created several leadership programs for young and mid-career professionals and is training more and more people in the basic principles of collaboration, communication and leadership. His blog/vlog can be found at LifeFraming.org and he resides in Indiana, PA with his wife and three children.

Made in the USA
Lexington, KY
24 February 2016